W9-AVT-245

*Dedicated in Memory of
Elizabeth and Frank Cordella,*

*My parents who always
encouraged me to succeed.*

**Hebron Public Library
201 W. Sigler Street
Hebron, IN 46341**

Hebron Public Library
201 W. Sigler Street
Hebron, IN 46341

www.mascotbooks.com

Teens and the Job Game (2nd Edition)

©2018 Beverly Slomka. All Rights Reserved. No part of this publication may be reproduced, stored in a retrieval system or transmitted in any form by any means electronic, mechanical, or photocopying, recording or otherwise without the permission of the author.

For more information, please contact:
Mascot Books
620 Herndon Parkway, Suite 320
Herndon, VA 20170
info@mascotbooks.com

Library of Congress Control Number: 2017916224

CPSIA Code: PBANG0118A
ISBN-13: 978-1-68401-547-4

Printed in the United States

TEENS *and the*
JOB GAME
Prepare Today—Win It Tomorrow

Porter County Public Library

Hebron Public Library
201 W. Sigler Street
Hebron, IN 46341

habnf   HEB
331.702 SLOMK

Slomka, Beverly
Teens and the job game
33410014991493   09/21/18

DISCARD

PORTER COUNTY LIBRARY SYSTEM

Beverly Slomka, MSEd

An Inspiring Guide for Developing Your Whole Person
Today and Winning the Job of Your Dreams Tomorrow

Table of Contents

Acknowledgments

There are many people who helped bring life to this book. I would like to thank all of those whom I interviewed and who are quoted and/or mentioned in the book. Their experience and testimony are living proof of the book's message.

I also want to thank Sister Mary Ellen Vesey, an inspiring Catholic chaplain who gave me the idea for the *Reflections* after each chapter. I want to thank Marilyn McHugh, a great friend who helped edit the chapters as I wrote them, and helped me find the right words when I couldn't say it just right.

I want to thank my managers at Merrill Lynch & Co., particularly Roger M. Vasey, retired executive vice president. Roger was a superb mentor and taught me a great deal about the workplace, about work ethic, and how to be the best employee.

I want to thank those who read the manuscript and offered their encouragement throughout the process, especially Helen Barra, and my "angel" Carol Carmellino. Finally, I want to thank my husband, Edward, for his patience and encouragement through the long hours I spent writing this book. Thank you, Ed, for cheering me on.

Introduction

You are probably wondering what this "job game" is all about.
You might have chosen this book because you are looking for
a part-time or summer job while in high school, or maybe a
parent or teacher asked you to read it. If someone gave you
this book to read, you may be wondering why you have to think
about work now while you are a teenager in high school. You
might be thinking that your studies are enough to think about
now, and I'm sure you are involved in many outside activities
that take up a lot of your time.

As a young adult, you are probably very involved with your
friends and looking forward to weekends and time out of school
to relax and enjoy yourself.

I know that it is difficult to look too far ahead when you are
enmeshed in so many activities, and that's okay. It certainly is
important to focus on your studies and other school activities,
and parts of this book will reinforce the importance of this
aspect in this stage of your life, but it is also important to enjoy
friends and your favorite out-of-school activities.

As someone who has had three careers and been involved
in recruitment for many years, I know there is another very
important aspect of your life that you must focus on now along
with your studies and your relationships.

Despite the many activities that take up your time, you must begin to look beyond today and begin to develop your image, your *whole person*, for the world of work tomorrow.

Your whole person is the one that a future employer will meet and examine closely when you apply for volunteer work, for the summer job you want, or for the job of your dreams in the future.

The act of searching for work and being successful in the workplace can be compared to a complex game that presents you with many challenges along the way—challenges to your skills, your ethics, your judgment, and your attitudes. That is why I call it *the job game*. To win at this game you must begin today, and not wait until after high school or college, to develop yourself for the workplace.

This is not your usual job-hunting book. It is a short book that you can read in one sitting if you wish, and you will want to refer back to for information and inspiration. It will not focus heavily on resume writing or job interview questions. These topics will be covered to the extent that you will need them.

Preparing a resume and preparing for the job interview will take, at most, several hours of your time; however, forming your whole person is a growth process that takes place over a number of months or years. Therefore, this is something you must start *now*.

Throughout this book I will guide you in taking your first steps. By beginning to focus on developing your whole person today, you will be well on your way to meeting the challenges of work.

Your high school studies are preparing you with the necessary hands-on skills for work. I realize that there is great emphasis in schools today on standardized tests, but even these tests prepare the student for the necessary pre-college tests—the SATs and ACTs, as well as other college skills.

However, the development of your complete person depends, not only on your study skills and test results, but also on everything about you that you see in yourself and that others in the world see in you. It includes your dress, your speech, your deportment, your feelings and attitudes, your skills and interests, and your relationships with others.

Maybe you are not headed to a four-year college. Perhaps you are planning on going to a community college or trade school based on a particular work interest. In fact, there is more discussion today for the need for more vocational training, as there are shortages in many trades—construction and plumbing—for example.

Work in these and other areas are just as important and can be just as fulfilling as careers that depend on a college education. For those of you preparing to go into a trade, preparing for the workplace is even more imperative at this point. The image that you begin to develop as a teenager will be carried into college or other training school and beyond, to form the person you ultimately will become.

Joseph Slomka, Jr. is my nephew and a graduate of the Master's program in color science from the Rochester Institute of Technology. Color science is a highly technical subject.

Color scientists study how people perceive color and how it is applied to the manufacture of color products. Color scientists are sought after by companies specializing in motion picture development and photography, and by manufacturers of plastics, cosmetics, computers, and printers.

Joe told me about his attempts to find his first job during his undergraduate years. Despite his talents he found that it was not enough to have the specialized skills he had acquired in school to find an appropriate first job. He did not realize the importance of presentation skills and self-confidence until he went through at least ten job interviews without receiving a job offer.

Eventually, he realized he would have to develop his communication skills in order to adequately convey his work skills and talents. Ultimately, he understood the need to prepare his *whole person.*

You are on the threshold of the rest of your life. Work, no matter how lofty or how humble, is a necessary part of life. Each chapter in this book will take you to another level of preparation for the workplace. In the first chapter, you will be asked to reflect on your current image, including your physical presence and your feelings about yourself, your studies, and your future work.

The remaining chapters will relate your life in school today to your future work, and will give you some practical guidelines on how to choose your career, how to search for your first job, and how to ultimately succeed in the workplace.

You will be inspired by other teens and successful young men and women as they reinforce what you need to succeed in the workplace. Following each chapter, there will be a *Reflections* section that will give you the opportunity to think about and write down your feelings and actions about the concepts discussed.

My hope is that this book will help you to meet head-on the challenges you will face in approaching the world of work. With real life examples, you will learn that you can be successful, even if you may not be a top student. While you should always strive to do your best, this book is for those students who may struggle as well as for those who are doing well.

I can assure you that as a recruiter I have discovered, as has my nephew Joe, that it is not only the resume and the tangible skills that you bring to the workplace that count, but the intangibles as well. In the competitive world we live in today, you must stand out, and this book provides the tools you will need to become a unique, whole person with well-rounded skills to win at the job game.

Looking Back . . .

I can't believe I was once where you are today. It went so fast. One day I was in high school with all of the dreams that you might have today. Now I've completed many years in the workforce, and for the past ten years, I have been recruiting healthcare personnel. What a ride it has been!

When I was in high school, the future was like an open field where I could become anything I wanted. I don't remember if I really thought about how I would attain my dreams, except that I knew I wanted to go to college and have a career.

I focused on school and enjoyed it, although some subjects were difficult for me. Along with the challenging subjects and worries about tests, I made some lifelong friends and also had some fun. School seemed never-ending at that time, and work seemed far away. I don't think that I consciously looked at myself as part of the equation for succeeding in life, and until junior year I had only a vague idea of what I wanted to do in life.

When I had completed junior year I decided, or thought I had decided, on my career. I liked working with people and helping people. I decided I wanted to be a psychologist. As with many of us who have great plans, things turned out differently.

The road that led to where I spent most of my work life was not a straight one. It changed course as I passed my teenage years through my twenties and beyond. My work journey was shaped by changing interests and life experiences. Therefore, what happened over the two and a half decades past my teens was not what I expected, but it turned out to be more exciting, and provided many life lessons about the workplace.

I would like to take you on a brief journey through my work history to share some of these lessons and to unveil some of the secrets of succeeding in the workplace. Looking back with me will set the stage for you to look ahead.

After graduating high school, I went on to college to receive my BA in psychology. In my senior year of college, I decided that instead of going for a Ph.D. in psychology, I would pursue a relatively new career in rehabilitation counseling. I went on to get my MS in education in rehabilitation counseling.

Rehabilitation counselors work with mentally or physically disabled persons, or persons recovering from substance abuse. The goal is to bring those individuals to the point where they can go back to the workforce. I was really excited to begin my career.

When I finally graduated with my degree in 1976, New York City was in the midst of a fiscal crisis. I couldn't find a job. I have to explain that I am a petite woman, about five feet tall. I didn't give the first employers I encountered the impression that I had the potential to take on a heavyweight drug abuser or severely mentally challenged person. It was very difficult to land that first job.

As it turned out, I married shortly after I received my graduate degree, and even though my husband worked in a government job, we really needed two salaries. I had to begin looking outside of my field of interest and try to find at least a temporary job.

I went to an employment firm and was placed in an administrative assistant position with a child-care advocacy agency. The agency, which probably exists today in a different form and under a different name, worked closely with New York State and New York City officials and other agencies.

Its mission was to guarantee optimum care and funding for the various child-care agencies throughout the state of New York. I thought I would just stay for a few months. As it turned out, I stayed for four years. It was not what I first set out to do, but it was a wonderful place to work.

I would not use my counseling skills on this job. All it required was the typing skill that I had acquired in high school, the ability to help coordinate the agency's activities, and the aptitude to work well with my managers and co-workers. It was the beginning of my workplace experience, and I began to learn what work was all about.

I'll fast forward now through my next two careers. After four years in the child-care advocacy agency, I was twenty-eight years old. I suddenly wanted to do something completely different. I had an attraction to the corporate world.

My next position was in Merrill Lynch & Co., a large financial services company, now part of Bank of America. When I joined Merrill Lynch, I had no financial experience, but since I had worked as an administrative assistant in the child-care agency, I was offered a senior secretarial position.

I was told that, based on my education and past experience, accepting this job could eventually lead to a more professional position. I took the job although I was overqualified. Within three months, I became the administrative assistant, and within three years I became assistant vice president of administration in a growing department.

Within another three years, I became vice president in a major division. Eventually, I was vice president and administrative manager of a sector comprised of over one thousand employees, and I eventually moved to other divisions and departments along the way.

As part of my administrative responsibilities throughout my career at Merrill Lynch, I managed administrative staff and recruited staff at all levels. I recruited college graduates and MBA candidates for analyst and associate positions. I recruited summer help, mid-level professionals, and other administrative staff.

After twenty-two years of a successful, enjoyable, and hectic career—one that I had never imagined—I was beginning to think of a change. After witnessing the World Trade Center attack, I decided to reduce my workload.

I was interested in pursuing work in the health care field. Over the years, my own health issues and those of my family spurred my interest in health care.

I secured my first health care position as a hospital Concierge in the private treatment unit of a major medical center. For the third time in my working career, I was overqualified for the position, but I knew it was a position that would help me learn about the workings of a hospital. I knew I could always move up in the future.

After seven months in the Concierge position, I was promoted to supervisor of the concierge and hostess staff on this special unit. Patients there paid an additional fee to be in a more hotel-like environment, with hostess and concierge service throughout the day.

The mission of the staff was to ensure patients were comfortable and received the meals they requested, and to offer additional amenities to add to the comfortable environment. During my time in this position, various staff and scheduling changes took place. This is how I got to meet *Ms. Jones* and this is where your journey begins.

1

Taking a Good Look at Yourself—Part One of the Strategy to Win at the Job Game

THE STORY OF MS. JONES

Although I had recruited and managed staff for many years, the pressures of Wall Street did not allow me the time to focus on what makes some potential employees more attractive to an employer than others. I knew a good employee when I saw one, but I never thought of putting a label on the full embodiment of a good employee.

In my new supervisory position on the hospital unit, I was more relaxed, and finally able to realize that it is one's whole person that comes to interview for the job, and the employer's perception of a current or potential employee depends on how well that person has prepared his or her entire self for the job.

I confronted the whole person issue when one of my part-time weekend hostesses was preparing to go back to school and I needed to hire a replacement. I was pleased when one of my staff recommended a hospital volunteer who had helped the staff on the unit and was considered to be a good worker.

I contacted this young volunteer, who was about nineteen years old and had just finished her first year of college. I looked forward to meeting her and made an appointment with her for a formal interview. I was confident that my search for a hostess would be over once we had met, since she came highly recommended.

Ms. Jones came to the interview, and the first thing I noticed was that she was very neat and had a warm smile. Upon further inspection, I noticed she was wearing jeans. I was disappointed that she did not realize that this was a formal interview and could have used better judgment on what to wear. After I had secured a private space to interview Ms. Jones, I asked her if she had a resume or work history to present to me. Ms. Jones had no resume or any type of paperwork. That was disappointment number two.

Ms. Jones seemed calm, but it was very difficult for me to learn about her. She answered questions with very short answers, her voice was very low, and she had no questions about the job. I did learn that she was in college and studying to be a nurse.

I told her about the job, and the need for her to be flexible regarding her work hours and dealing with sometimes very ill or difficult patients. I also told her that the job could be very rewarding. I then invited a senior hostess to come into the room and interview her and give Ms. Jones the opportunity to ask the senior hostess questions about the job. Ms. Jones did not ask any questions.

I could not hire Ms. Jones. Although she came highly recommended, she was totally unprepared for the interview. Her dress, her communication skills, her preparation, and her performance in the interview were all lacking. The senior hostess who also interviewed her agreed with me.

I needed to feel confident that the person I hired would speak with confidence and compassion to patients and would add value to the unit. I was sorry that I could not hire Ms. Jones. Because Ms. Jones could not communicate her person to me, I did not have enough information about her as a worker to hire her in this very people-oriented job.

Employees today are prepared in academics, but not necessarily for the real world. Young people need to take control of their future.

Luz King, Information, Security Analyst

I am giving you a heads-up. I'm sure you don't want to be in the same position as Ms. Jones. This is why I'm encouraging you to look ahead and beyond your everyday thoughts and activities, and begin looking at your total self as a means to realize your dreams.

If you agree to take a hard look at your image outside and inside, and recognize that developing your whole person is an important part of your preparation for the future workplace, you will not be like Ms. Jones. Ms. Jones was a bright young lady with great potential. She had taken an important step in volunteering in a hospital, a step that would give her more understanding of her future career. Yet, she was not prepared to interview for work.

YOUR IMAGE TODAY

What image do you think you present to others? Do you ever look at yourself in the mirror when you dress, and think about the image you present to the world—in school, with your friends, and on social media?

I know you must look at the image you present to your fellow students. I understand the pressures you must face in high school to be like others, to dress in the latest fashions, and have the latest hairstyle or jewelry or shoes. There is nothing wrong with being stylish; however, different styles will present different images to the world.

Do you ever think how you communicate to your peers, your parents, or your teachers? What is your attitude toward your studies? Do you just want to *get by*, or are you truly interested in your studies and trying to do your best?

What if someone came to you and offered you a weekend job or a volunteer job in the profession you are interested in pursuing in the future? Would you be prepared?

The image you present to the employer, whether for a volunteer or paid position, is one that tells the employer about your whole person. Your dress, your speech, how you walk, sit down at an interview, present yourself, and ask questions conveys to the employer what kind of person you are.

You cannot change your image overnight when it is time to go on a job interview. Rather, you will either present the image you are today, or the new image you begin to prepare today. What do you think an employer will think of the person you see in the mirror today?

It is not really difficult to begin molding an attractive and polished image. Nevertheless, it may take some boldness and courage in the face of the pressures that come from your peers in person and online.

Boldness (not the bullying kind, but rather the feeling of confidence) and courage, themselves, are attributes that you will need as you move ahead to face the challenges of the workplace.

THE IMPORTANCE OF YOUR PHYSICAL PRESENCE

Let's start with your dress. The way you are dressed provides the first image of your person. As I just mentioned, in your everyday life you can be stylish without wearing scruffy pants or jeans. If you want to truly stand out to a future employer, and to your friends as well, you can wear something stylish, but not provocative or sloppy.

When I went to college, I never wore jeans. I could never get them to fit right! As a petite person, I didn't have as many clothing choices as I have today. There was very little clothing sold in petite sizes, and in jeans, petite sizes were just about nonexistent. As a result, I bought stylish chinos, corduroys, or woolen pants, depending on the season. Sometimes, I even had to go to the preteen department to buy clothes!

I persisted in wanting to look good. I wore the latest styles, made sure the various items were a good match, and somehow, I received compliments on the way I dressed.

There is nothing wrong with jeans. Jeans can be dressy in some ways if worn with the right shirt, blouse, or sweater; however, jeans are not appropriate for a job interview. They're certainly fine with your friends after school or work, but sloppy, torn, or jeans that are too long are just not attractive at any time. If you are an attractive person, do you realize that you actually hide your good looks when your clothes are sloppy?

I'm not being your parent here, or preaching to you, so please don't put the book down. I'm writing to you from my heart about how I see the image of the student today from the perspective of being a manager and a recruiter. I feel strongly that the youth of today need to make a difference in the world. You need to show the world that you are the future leaders, movers, and shakers.

It was not immediately apparent to me as I went through my careers that my appearance had a lot to do with how my future would unfold. As time went on, and I grew in experience, it became obvious that I had not been hired and promoted along the way just because of experience or intellect.

I learned that the way I dressed, spoke, and presented myself in general were part of the secret. The manager who hired me for my first job in health care told me after I was hired that he knew I would be the right person for the job because of the way I dressed and presented myself. Remember, I had just left the financial services field and had no health care experience.

I always dressed well in high school and college.
When you dress well, you feel good.

Maria Reyes, Financial Analyst

Maria Reyes, who came to the United States from the Dominican Republic when she was six years old, remembers watching two neighbors who went to work when she was still going to school. Maria admired how they were dressed and copied their way of dress throughout her schooling and into the workplace.

Maria is one of my former employees from Merrill Lynch who advanced from administrative assistant to senior-level accounting positions in major financial services and banking firms.

There is some great fashionable clothing that is available today for young men and women in your age group. If you want to be treated as an adult, take into consideration how your clothes can help convey a mature and professional appearance.

Experiment with something other than jeans. Try on clothes with different fabrics and colors that are neat and enhance your coloring and features. You will be pleasantly surprised at how great you look to yourself and others.

Dare to be different, and you will be practicing to win at the job game.

Some of our volunteers, both in high school and college, need to focus on strengthening their verbal and written communications skills.

Bonnie Olsen, Director of Volunteer Services (Retired)
Lutheran Medical Center, Brooklyn, New York

COMMUNICATION SAYS IT ALL

Employers are saying today that high school and college students really need to strengthen their communication skills. Along with a good appearance, good communication skills are very important. Communication skills are part of the first impression you will give employers when you apply for or interview for a job. What about your speech? How well do you speak?

I don't mean that you need to use big words or have a very large vocabulary. There is a proper way to speak: using an appropriate tone of voice, using correct grammar, and avoiding the use of slang.

Maybe you speak very well and are comfortable speaking with all sorts of people. Maybe sometimes you have difficulty finding the right words. If you are in the last category, better speech is something you can certainly develop.

Most high school curricula include several subjects that would provide an opportunity to enhance your communication skills. In addition, expanding your interest in what you want to read and view on TV and social media will help improve your communication skills, as well as give you confidence speaking among groups of people.

There's so much interesting information on all types of subjects available today, so that your ability to learn about many things in the world, and make you a more interesting and well-rounded person, is easier than ever.

People who can communicate well tend to be looked upon more positively when looking for a job, even if their skills still need to be developed.

William Hoyt, Embedded Software Engineer Associate, Lockheed Martin

I cannot begin to tell you how shy I was as a teenager. I was okay with my friends, but I was always a little fearful of my teachers, and with strangers it was even harder.

I did a little better in college. Going from a small private high school to a large city college intimidated me at first. It took some time to gain confidence. I didn't give up. I just persevered, and gulped, and forged ahead.

Gradually, I began to speak louder and with more confidence. Certainly, as I moved ahead in the work world, the way I spoke was a big factor in giving my manager confidence that I could conduct a meeting on his behalf, or negotiate with co-workers on important issues.

There was evidence that I was a Brooklynite, especially when I spoke with those who were born in Chicago or Boston or Manhattan; however, I became more aware of my speech, and spoke more slowly and carefully, so that my speech became more professional-sounding.

William Hoyt cannot say enough about the importance of good communication skills. William was a student at the Rochester Institute of Technology and was hired after graduation for a co-operative program at Lockheed Martin. William spoke to me about the importance of good communication.

He felt that communication skills can make a big difference in how a potential employee is viewed, even if he or she doesn't have all the skills for a job. After his internship, William was hired permanently at Lockheed Martin as an Embedded Software Engineer Associate. William is successful at his young age, and you can hear it in his voice, in the way he speaks.

You are learning proper English now through your high school education. Try to be aware of how you speak to others, and start now to use this proper English rather than slang. This is not to say you can't speak to your friends using the latest expressions. (Hopefully these expressions are not vulgar, because vulgarity is never acceptable in business.)

All generations have their expressions; however, in general, you should speak in such a way that you will be understood by everyone.

WHAT IS *DEPORTMENT*? WHY IS IT IMPORTANT?

Deportment is a very important part of a person's image. Deportment is the way you carry yourself.

This may be a word you haven't heard too often, if at all. It is not really a modern or up-to-date term, maybe because not many people today think about deportment. It means your overall behavior, manner, or posture. It includes your body language. This is very much a part of your whole person.

When you come into a room, any person you are facing sees your deportment in your manner of walking, your posture, your dress, and your way of speaking. It presents a first picture of your whole person.

Deportment can tell a person if you are nice, or confident, or arrogant, or sloppy. It can attract a person, or it can repel them.

For example, if you are interviewing for a volunteer position in a local community center, the manager who interviews you will know a great deal about you once you enter his or her office.

If you come into the office dressed neatly, walking with confidence, with a smile on your face, and you speak with enthusiasm, you have a better chance of getting that volunteer position than someone who comes to the interview with wrinkled pants, sneakers, who doesn't smile, and who walks with his or her head down.

Deportment really wraps up the whole person. The physical attributes just discussed—your dress and speech—are very much a part of it, but the more intangible parts, such as your feelings and cares and attitudes, form the rest of it.

YOUR FEELINGS AND ATTITUDES AND THE "SUCCESS EQUATIONS"

I got my first job because I had confidence. I talked to myself, and felt positive about myself. This helped me in the interview.

Danese Giacchino, NYC School Teacher

I know that as a young adult you have a lot of different feelings. You feel strongly and differently about many things, and you are entitled to your feelings. There are some feelings and attitudes that are more important in helping develop your whole person.

If those feelings or attitudes in some way take you away from the important things in your life right now, some work needs to be done to address this.

The most important feeling you have is how you feel about yourself. Do you feel good about yourself? If you do, this will help you on the way to building further confidence. Danese Giacchino was a junior in high school when she obtained her first part-time job.

Danese told me that what helped her in her first job interview was her self-confidence. When I asked her how she gained self-confidence, she told me that it was the feeling she had within herself. She felt "positive" about herself and looked positive.

When it came time to interview for this job, Danese told herself that she could do it. Although she was nervous at her first interview, she got the job. Her confidence started with good feelings about herself.

If for some reason you don't feel good about yourself, this needs to be examined. Why don't you feel good about yourself? Is it due to family issues? Is it because of how your friends speak to you or view you? Is it that you just don't feel good about yourself, and you don't know why?

If you don't feel good about yourself, it is very important that you address this with someone you are comfortable with. A parent would be a good start. If you don't want to, or can't speak with a parent, you need to seek someone's help.

Think about speaking to a guidance counselor, a teacher that you like, a best friend's parent, a religious leader, or other professional that you trust. You must address this first and foremost—now.

If your bad feelings are only a temporary teenage *funk* with you feeling unhappy about your date the other night, that's not the issue I'm talking about. The important thing is that you usually feel good about yourself. Maybe you're not happy or thrilled with life every day, but feeling good about yourself means that you are comfortable with yourself and with your life in general. That's how it should be.

Along with your feelings go your attitudes. Do you have a good attitude about life in general and about your friends and family? Do you carry a chip on your shoulder?

Are things not going well at home, and as a result you take it out on other people—or do you smile a lot and usually behave pleasantly toward others? How do you approach people? Do you show respect and caring?

Attitudes, like feelings, are based on your experiences. Your experiences in life will be good, bad, and somewhere in between. The way you approach these experiences will form your feelings and attitudes as you journey through life. You can buckle under the weight of major family problems or concerns, or you can address and face them, by yourself or with help.

Once again, if there are major issues in your life affecting the way you feel, affecting your attitudes, and affecting your studies, they need to be addressed. Do not be afraid to seek counseling or support from good friends, family members you respect, or professionals.

My mother died when I was fourteen, a few months into my first year of high school. My sister was married, and I was left with my father who could not be immediately supportive, as he was so overwhelmed with grief. My friends were initially uncomfortable about the death, and avoided me.

Thankfully, I had a rather large family who were very supportive and helped me through it, but it took time. I also felt that God had a reason for this, and I pledged to do my best to meet the challenges of suddenly becoming a homemaker as well as being a student.

I coped on the outside by seeking out my friends, writing poems, and listening to my favorite music, but I harbored a lot of anxiety inside. It was not popular to seek counseling in the 1960s. I leaned on my sister and wonderful aunts and uncles who helped me through it all.

In my college years, I did seek counseling because I didn't want to be crippled by ongoing anxiety. It was one of the best things I ever did in my life. It helped me forge through many other challenges, and it was sometimes amazing how I could cope through bad times. I found out that time heals, and my father also found his peace.

In life, as in algebra, there are equations. I call them "success equations."

Feeling good about yourself = valuing and respecting yourself = confidence.

Valuing yourself leads to valuing other people + having a good attitude toward others = building strong relationships.

The workplace is full of relationships. Success in workplace relationships results from valuing yourself + valuing others.

It is important to take note of your feelings and attitudes and examine whether you need some help. A good feeling inside, and a positive attitude toward life and relationships, go a long way toward helping one be successful. It is what I call *the success equations.*

Good feelings about yourself equal valuing and respecting yourself, and this equals confidence. Valuing yourself leads you to value others, and this builds relationships. The workplace is full of relationships. The better you feel about yourself, the better your attitude, and the better you will work and foster good working relationships.

What you give out from your person, you will get back. It may seem simplistic to tell you how important it is for you to smile a lot. As simple as it is, a smiling countenance is very important when meeting an employer and interacting in the workplace. It is part of your general deportment. It speaks volumes about your confidence, positive feelings, and attitudes. It makes others feel comfortable, and it makes you feel even better.

YOUR FEELINGS ABOUT SCHOOL

The importance of your feelings and attitudes about school and your studies is right behind the feelings about yourself. Your attitude about your studies is one of the most important aspects of your life today.

If you don't care how you are doing in school, you cannot look forward to doing well in the workplace. If you are truly determined to do well, even in the face of challenging subjects, you will ultimately succeed.

Study requires discipline and hard work. These are two things that are necessary not only in the workplace but in the way you live your whole life. As the saying goes, *there is no free lunch.*

This does not mean that you must struggle throughout your life to achieve success in your work or personal life. I don't want to paint a picture of drudgery or lack of enjoyment, because discipline and hard work actually bring about the opposite. I simply mean that you need to appropriately prioritize certain aspects of your life in order to succeed.

Most young people do not like discipline, either from their parents or from school; however, it is a necessary building block for life. Discipline and hard work based on sound values ultimately bring you freedom, contentment, success, and many other good things. I will talk about this more in the next chapter when I illustrate the important link between school and the workplace.

YOUR FEELINGS ABOUT WORK

Do you have definite feelings about the workplace? If you have had a job or volunteered, you probably have formed some feelings, including likes and dislikes. Whatever work you will do throughout your life, you must approach that work with the right feelings and attitudes.

As we will discuss in Chapter Five, attitude is one of the most important elements in job success and employee happiness. We will examine workplace issues, so that you can approach future work with an understanding of the work environment, can learn how to approach different work environments, and can discover your role within the workplace.

IDENTIFYING YOUR FUTURE WORK GOAL

It's important that students in high school begin thinking about where they are going. They have to find out who they are and take an active role in their future.

Dennis Straub, Former 12th Grade Physics Teacher, current Aeronautical engineer

Have you thought about what type of work you want to do? Are you thinking of college? Have you chosen your major? Maybe you have, but maybe you don't quite know yet.

Life experiences and interests lead all of us to choose the type of career we pursue. If you don't know what you want to do just yet, you can begin by thinking about your interests. Begin to ask yourself these questions: *What interests me? What makes me curious about life? What do I hear about or know that makes me want to find out more? Are there things that I do extremely well—things that I love to do? What can I picture myself doing after school is finished? How do I see myself ten years from now?*

Whatever you might be interested in today, whether it is law, medicine, financial services, computer science, music, sales, firefighting, etc., you should begin to investigate this interest now.

In Chapter Three, I will explain how you can begin to investigate your interests and to identify your future goals. I will discuss the importance of volunteer work or internships related to a potential career goal to give you a more practical view of this goal. I'll give you additional practical guidelines on identifying an appropriate job goal and pursuing your interest while you are still in high school.

As a high school student, you are at the crossroads of the rest of your life. When you go to college or to a vocational school, you should already be on your way to your future career. The way you examine your image and develop your person now will serve you for the rest of your life.

If you can answer the questions I have posed in this chapter honestly, you will begin to discover more of yourself. If you can act on the personal issues you see in your life today, and seek help to solve your problems if you need it, you will feel good about yourself and will find confidence. It's up to you.

Your future person is in your hands. Now is the time to act, as you approach the next stage of your life with a view to achieving your dreams and goals.

REFLECTIONS

Write down some of the major feelings you have from day to day.

_____

_____

_____

If you sometimes don't feel good about yourself, how do you cope with this?

_____

_____

_____

What is your attitude about life today? How do you feel about your family and friends?

_____

_____

_____

Do you smile a lot? If not, why not?

_____

_____

_____

What is it that might make you feel better about yourself or those around you?

_____

_____

What actions will you take to improve your feelings and attitudes?

_____

_____

_____

How do you think your feelings and attitudes are important in finding and keeping work in the future, and in helping to meet your future goals?

_____

_____

_____

What do you envision yourself doing in the future?

_____

_____

_____

What steps do you think you need to take to reach your future goal?

_____

_____

_____

2

Your Education and the Workplace—
How They are Linked

As a freshman, you make a choice of where you are going in life.
It's important to apply yourself and prioritize.

Ashley Smith, 18, high school senior,
now Assistant Director of Policy & Planning,
NYC Health and Hospitals Correctional Health

YOUR STUDIES—YOUR WORK OF TODAY

You probably don't realize that, as a student, you are actually
at work today. You went through elementary school as a child,
growing up and beginning to learn about the world. You know
much more now, and you are facing more challenges, as you go
through your high school years.

You are facing personal challenges, school challenges, social challenges, and parental challenges; however, when you go to school five days a week, you are doing the work of a young adult.

What you do in school, and how you study and prepare yourself before and after school, is your work of today. Therefore, how you apply yourself to your studies today will have a direct effect on how you approach future work.

ARE YOU DOING WELL IN SCHOOL? IF NOT, HOW TO MAKE IT BETTER

How are you doing in school? Maybe you are doing well in some subjects and not in others. I'm sure you are beginning to see your strengths and weaknesses. How are you approaching the subjects that are more difficult? Do you sometimes feel you'll never get through them?

When you finally reach the workplace, you will have the same feelings. There will be challenges and you will wonder whether you will succeed or not. The basic formula for success in school and in the workplace is very simple: *Apply yourself and persist.*

If you are in the right school and classes for your abilities, and if you are in the right job, based on your skills and abilities, there is almost nothing you cannot do if you apply yourself and persist in learning.

Education is key. Having the right skills is important.

Jose Hernandez, Regional Traffic Operations Manager, Virginia Department of Transportation

You might be doing very well in school and feel that you are not challenged very much. Or, you may really be struggling and afraid you will fail a course or two.

Like most students, you may be somewhere in between these two extremes, feeling good about some subjects and not liking others. You might be anxious about or have difficulty with the standardized tests that are so integral to education today.

When we talked about feelings in the first chapter, I stressed the importance of addressing any bad feelings you may have about yourself. This also applies to problems in school. If you are having difficulty in school, speak to your teachers, your parents, and your guidance counselor.

Most schools today should have a tutoring and mentoring program, or your teachers could help guide you through the tough spots. In addition, there are several outside tutoring services that can help. Through it all, it is important that you persist in trying to learn and understand those subjects that are difficult for you.

My challenges were math and physics. I had particular difficulty with physics. I just couldn't get it. I studied and paid attention in class, but I thought I was lost. I persisted in trying to understand it, and one day the light bulb finally went on in my head!

It suddenly made sense to me. I couldn't believe it! I can still remember where I was sitting when it all just started to make sense. After that, I enjoyed the class and actually passed the New York State Physics Regents exam, a New York State standardized test, with a 90 percent.

This could happen to you. In many cases, if you are having

difficulty in a class, and you persist in trying to learn, and seek help along the way, it could all come together for you in the end. Never give up.

You need to approach difficult subjects with a positive, can-do attitude. Tell yourself that you must and will do well.

Dennis Straub, Former 12th Grade Physics Teacher, current Aeronautical Engineer

Perceptions and attitudes toward certain subjects also have an effect on how well you do in class. Dennis Straub told me that he was a biological sciences major at the University of Pittsburgh. He told me that one of his problem subjects in college was organic chemistry. He had heard from other students how hard this subject was and he went into the class feeling that he would not do well.

In fact, he did poorly, getting a D in the subject. He took the class again at a later time, feeling that he must do better and determined that he would do better. The next time he got an A+. When I spoke with Dennis several years ago, he was a twelfth grade physics teacher, contemplating a career in medicine. Now, he is an aeronautical engineer.

THE ESSENTIAL SKILLS OF TIME MANAGEMENT AND ORGANIZATION

Whether or not you are having difficulties, and even if you are breezing through your studies, it is very important that you always apply yourself to your studies and develop two important skills: time management and organizational skills.

Many students today are involved in several after-school activities. This will make your school day longer, so that when you come home it might be difficult to begin your homework. You need to manage your time very carefully, so that you can take part in sports and other after-school activities that you like and also do your studies.

Time management is key in school, and it is essential in the workplace. It helps you accomplish what must be done. If you haven't done so already, try to formulate a plan of study each day.

Address those subjects you find particularly difficult when you are refreshed and have the most energy. Don't put off the small assignments because they are small and easy. Get them out of the way to make room for the assignments that will take the most time.

Organize yourself. Make lists if that helps. At work and at home I make lists of what I need to do. Making lists has gone a long way toward helping me accomplish everything I need to within the necessary timeframe.

Organizing your life around studies and other personal interests also means prioritizing your work. If you have two deadlines, concentrate on the first deadline well ahead of time, but begin to think about the second deadline early on, so that you can jump on the work that must be done in a timely fashion.

I have encountered classmates and colleagues who don't pay attention to the appearance of their work. They hand in sloppy work to get it done fast. It is unacceptable!

Maria Reyes, Financial Analyst

The importance of organizing yourself is not only relevant to how you approach your studies but also to how you present your work. If you are doing a project, an essay, or a paper, it needs to be organized. The best way to organize a project or paper is to break it down into parts in your mind.

Think about the various elements or parts that will make up the whole project or paper, write them down, and then embellish each part to come up with the whole.

This is what you will need to do when you are in the workplace. No matter what project you are given, it will always be made up of various parts that, added together, will make up the whole.

Organizing your work also implies paying attention to neatness and detail. Lack of organization is a major issue in the workplace. Right behind lack of organization is lack of attention to details. You might have heard the expression: *It's all in the details.*

If you haven't heard this expression, I can tell you, *it is* all in the details. It's always the little details that get us into trouble. Lack of attention to detail in any type of work can mean the difference between passing and failing, or being a good employee or bad employee.

Imagine the young, newly hired employee taking an important

phone message and forgetting to give it to his/her boss. Would that go over very well? I could give you countless examples of issues that arise due to lack of attention to detail.

Instead, I am asking you to think about the way you do any of your school work, and to make sure that you pay attention to the finest detail, including the neatness of your work. Attention to detail and neat work are two other ways you present your image—your whole person—to a teacher or a boss.

Organizing yourself can also mean asking relevant questions about the assignments that you have. Take careful notes in school, and make a list of questions you might have about the assignment so that you can ask your teacher.

When you are given an assignment, make sure you understand the objective of the assignment. Never be afraid to ask questions. This is also essential in the workplace. It is far better to ask questions than to hand in a wrong assignment, or present your future boss with an incomplete or off-base presentation.

In almost any job, good employees go into their supervisor's office with a notepad ready to take notes, and have a list of questions and notes to discuss with their managers. It may seem like very simple advice, but keeping an organized notebook, jotting down questions, making lists, and prioritizing go a long way toward helping you complete an assignment and preparing you for the workplace.

If despite everything—applying yourself, managing your time, and organizing your work—you still find yourself struggling, you must do everything you can to work with your teachers and guidance staff to address this situation. Don't despair.

There are many stories of students who had a hard time in school, who went on to be very successful in careers. You just need to find your niche, and may have to do things a little differently than others. Once again, never be afraid to ask for help.

HOW TO LEVERAGE SUCCESS

> *Beware of the "Senior Slide." This is what happens when students begin to slack off in senior year when they are accepted in college. Students must realize that colleges will ask for a final transcript.*
>
> *Dennis Straub*, Former Physics Teacher,
> Current Aeronautical Engineer

If you are doing very well in school, you may feel more relaxed and in control of your coursework; however, you must never become lax. Once again, there is an important parallel to the workplace for those who do well.

If you complete an assignment well in the workplace, you must continue to use the same energy and interest in the next assignment. In school, if you are doing well in most subjects, you must continue to apply the same interest and energy in every subject.

Beware of what Dennis Straub calls the "senior slide," now more frequently referred to as *senioritis*. This is what he and other teachers had seen happen when seniors begin to receive college acceptances. They do well in the first part of the year, then slack off when the acceptances come in.

Dennis had seen "A" students become "C" students in certain subjects. You must realize that most colleges will ask for a final transcript as you graduate, and that a "C" grade will not look very good.

When you are successful in school, you can certainly use this success as leverage as you apply for work, however, you must never think that you won't have to work as hard to achieve your goals.

I have seen many Harvard graduates fall short on job interviews, or fall short on the job, because they were too confident and did not apply themselves completely to the preparation of the task.

Enjoy your success and fulfillment in school and beyond, but never take your eye off the ball!

DEVELOPING VERBAL AND WRITTEN COMMUNICATION SKILLS

The ability to express yourself, to speak and write well, is very important in the workplace.

Megan Bevan, Intermediate School Teacher

As I pointed out in the first chapter, good communication is an essential tool in applying for a job and in the workplace itself. Once again, your verbal communication skills are a key indicator of your whole person.

Verbal communication skills speak volumes in terms of your state of preparedness for the workplace. Writing skills fall right behind verbal communication skills, since most jobs require some type of writing skill.

> *You must be a good communicator; otherwise, you will wait for everything to come to you. You won't know how to ask for it, and in life and work, you can't wait for things to come to you.*

William Hoyt, Embedded Software Engineer Associate, Lockheed Martin

The development of both verbal and written communication skills should be covered in high school. English classes bring these communication skills to the forefront. While many of us take English classes for granted because we speak the language, English classes are very important to refine our speech and writing skills. For those of you whose native language is not English, you might find English classes more challenging.

If you are having difficulty in grasping the English language, you should seek information on the availability of language resources so that you can feel more comfortable with the language. I'm sure that as a foreign student, you more readily recognize the importance of learning to communicate well in your everyday life, as well as in preparation for the workplace.

Schools might have specific classes on writing or debating skills, or include these elements in English classes. The importance of your participation in writing and speech cannot be overstated. Your attention to speech and writing skills will spill over into every subject you take, and every assignment.

I know it is the age of texting and instant messaging, and while very convenient, it sometimes takes away from *real* communication. It may make developing good verbal communication skills more challenging.

When you get to the workplace, you may not realize that, depending on the job, you may be called on to participate in meetings, conference calls, or actually run a meeting.

You may become a supervisor or manager one day that will require you to use your communication skills to convey important information, and relate in a certain way to staff. Once again, developing good relationships is part of the workplace, and you will need to relate *in person* and on the phone to others and use diplomacy.

To increase your verbal communication skills, be an active participant in class. Take the opportunity to speak in class when appropriate. Speaking in front of the class helps build confidence, and it prepares you for future presentations you may have to make at work.

For some people, it's intimidating to speak in front of the class; however, the more you are afraid to do it, or the shyer you are, the more you must persist, and do it. It is only through doing it that you will gain the necessary confidence, and it will no longer be intimidating. In addition to speaking up in class, take assignments that may require a presentation in front of the class. Once again, it may be intimidating, but you must do it.

Developing good writing skills also takes work. Especially with the preponderance of text messaging, it's important to learn and practice "real" writing skills for the workplace. Once again, in the workplace, you may need to write memos, or compose e-mails that convey certain information with a certain tone.

The better your writing skills, the better you will be able to convey important things to your colleagues and management. As you write school papers, pay attention to your teachers' comments on your writing. If you have difficulty writing, speak to your teacher. There are books and other resources to help you write better.

Good writing skills and good verbal skills do not mean you have to use big words. You just need to use good grammar and be able to express an idea in a clear and concise way. Specific resources on verbal and written communication skills are listed in the *Suggested Reading and Resources* section at the end of this book.

THE IMPORTANCE OF DEVELOPING PROBLEM-SOLVING SKILLS

While you are in the midst of your high-school studies, you are constantly using your mind to memorize and solve problems. Solving problems, and developing and completing projects, are essential building blocks for the tasks of the workplace. It is not easy to solve problems. Human nature makes all of us want to take the easy way out. We want things to be easy for us. It's much more comfortable.

According to Megan Bevan, a middle school teacher, the ability to teach yourself something and accept the challenge of solving problems builds essential skills for the workplace. You might wonder why you have to take chemistry when your goal is to become an accountant. First of all, education provides a window to life and what makes up life in all its parts. Chemistry is part of life. Also, taking chemistry helps develop and sharpen your thinking ability, so that as you go through life, chemistry and other difficult subjects are the basis for fully developing your critical thinking skills.

In today's workplaces, *critical thinking skills* has become a common catch phrase in a list of job requirements. When you have to work extra hard to understand something, it actually challenges your thinking skills. The element of persistence comes in at this point, and if you persist, you will be rewarded with the result.

I'm sure you would agree that whenever you succeed in something difficult, it is much more rewarding. So, embracing the hardest subjects with gusto is the surest way to fully develop your critical thinking skills, and add more substance to your whole person.

A WORD ABOUT PEER PRESSURE

It may or may not seem strange to talk about peer pressure at this point; however, I'm sure that most of the friends you have today are your high school friends. I'm sure you will also agree that your friends have great influence on you, and you on them. Your friends, the pressure you receive from them, and the pressure you receive from other sources (online, texting, Facebook, etc.) are probably greater now than you will ever experience.

As I stated in the introduction, you are on the threshold of the rest of your life. You are on the threshold of adult life, with all of its freedoms and responsibilities. How you use these freedoms has very much to do with your sense of responsibility.

If you want to be treated as an adult and want to have an image that says to someone that you are an adult, you must act in a personally and socially responsible way in the choices you make and in whatever you do.

The key to resist peer pressure and focus on school is to be in the right environment—to associate with the right students who are helpful and self-motivated. I also keep myself busy and involved in sports.

Daniel Sanbeg, as a former High School Student

I know that peer pressure can result in distractions in school; tempt you not to study, to stay out late, or maybe sometimes even miss school. In addition, you may also be pressured to smoke, drink, take some type of drug, or have sex at a young age. It is very stressful for you; however, if you do everything else right in school, but you make a wrong choice or act irresponsibly, it will affect the rest of your life.

This doesn't mean that if you did try drugs, but stopped, or if you had sex and already had a child or fathered a child, you can't move ahead in life. I am not judging you. You are a precious, unique person who has a special purpose in the world. Yet, I am sure you know that your life has changed, maybe radically, and how you move ahead may be somewhat limited by the choices you once made. We all learn from our experiences, and we can all move ahead again, despite the detour in the road.

Daniel Sanbeg was sixteen years old and doing well in high school when I first spoke with him. He told me that while he was in middle school he was distracted by others, and it was very stressful for him. He even felt tormented by some.

In order to focus on his studies, he associated with friends who were helpful and self-motivated. In high school, Daniel continued to be in an environment of good friends and kept busy in sports.

Most importantly, and on a very personal note, you are all aware about the heartbreaking trend in bullying online. It is not only unacceptable on social media, but it shows the most complete disrespect of a young person.

Although social media didn't exist when I was in high school, I was a victim of bullying for several years. Being a darker skinned Mediterranean-type white person with buck teeth that needed braces, the taunting and name-calling started when I was in elementary school almost all the way up to the time I graduated.

The braces ultimately fixed my teeth, but the taunting left me with extremely low confidence and shyness. I never felt that I was attractive, and this persisted almost through my twenties. I eventually overcame it, but it was not easy.

For those who are victims of bullying, you need to realize that those bullying you are not the only people in your life, and you have to surround yourself with all those friends and acquaintances who value you as a person.

Many friends will come and go, and instead of taking in the bullying, you need to align yourself with others and not despair. The bullies will eventually go away, and you will make new friends.

If you are experiencing bullying, please visit *www.pacerteens againstbullying.org*. Remember that you are a unique, special person, and no one can take that away from you, no matter what.

You need to think about what you really want out of life.
When I was twenty, I worked hard, but I also partied a lot.
I was going in the wrong direction. Then I realized I would not achieve
my goals, or have the things I wanted until I straightened myself out.

Robert Tutrone, Owner, CR Landscaping

Since this book is about developing your whole person for the workplace, the way you handle peer pressure will be another way you shape the image you present to others. It is a very competitive world. You must stand out as having your whole person together; having a value system, a set of skills, an organized way to approach life, and a deportment that says *I have it together.*

I cannot tell you how to live your life, but I can tell you that the teenage years go quickly, and then you are suddenly in your twenties with a whole new set of goals in life. I can only ask you to think about how good it will feel to have it together.

You will walk down the street, or through the hallways of school, with confidence, knowing that you are a unique person, that you are open to the challenge, and that you dare to be different.

REFLECTIONS

How do you feel about school on a day-to-day basis? What is it about school that you like and dislike?

_____

_____

_____

What subjects are you having difficulty with?

_____

_____

_____

What is it about these subjects that you find difficult?

_____

_____

_____

What will you do to improve your understanding of these subjects?

_____

_____

_____

Are you an organized person? If not, list what steps you can take to make yourself more organized.

_____

_____

_____

Are you able to finish your assignments on time? If not, what gets in your way?

_____

_____

_____

List at least three things you can change in your life to make yourself more organized and to give yourself more time for studies and assignments.

_____

_____

_____

How do you feel about speaking in class, or before a crowd? Are you comfortable, or would you rather not do it?

_____

_____

_____

Based on what you read in Chapter Two, what steps will you take to make yourself more comfortable speaking up?

_____

_____

_____

What peer pressures are you feeling? How are you dealing with them?

_____

_____

_____

What steps do you think you can take to avoid negative peer pressure and take more responsibility as a unique person?

_____

_____

_____

If you have been able to resist peer pressure, think about the advice you can give to friends or others to make them understand the importance of taking responsibility for their lives.

_____

_____

_____

3
—

How to Choose a Career—Beginning Early
to Discover Your Niche in the World

If you don't enjoy what you do, it's not worth doing.
You have to love what you do in life.

William Hoyt, Embedded Software,
Engineer Associate, Lockheed Martin

When a person thinks about what he or she wants to become in life, it has a lot to do with his or her life experience at that point.

Some of you may want to follow in the footsteps of your parents or other relatives who have careers that are interesting or lucrative. Others may want to do something completely different from their family members. In either case, it is never too early to begin to think seriously about your career.

If you are a young female, even though you may contemplate marriage and children down the road, it is likely you will still spend a number of years working—both when you are single and if or when you are married.

For young men, even though the role of *breadwinner* may not be as relevant today, since most wives and mothers work, your role as a worker in the family is still very critical. No matter what your age, gender, or stage in life, work will be an essential part of it. Therefore, as William Hoyt says, *it is important that whatever you choose to do, you should love what you do.*

Adults spend most of their waking lives working, and if you are not happy in what you do, it can be miserable for you, and you will make co-workers miserable.

If you haven't yet thought about your career, it is time to discover your niche in the world. Just as looking at your image today and examining your feelings and attitudes are important, beginning to think about your career and the type of work you want to do are critical steps in forming your whole person.

Career = Skills + Interests + Personality

The right career for you will comprise the correct interpretation of your skills, your interests, and your personality. You need to begin by thinking of what interests you today, and picturing what type of work you can see yourself doing in the future.

Explore your interests. If you have many different interests, start to narrow them down to what seems most realistic to you based on your personality and abilities. Begin to do comprehensive research on these interests, making note of the requirements of your potential career, as well as the time commitment in terms of school and work.

If nothing seems to strike you immediately, make an appointment to see your guidance counselor or speak with a teacher you admire to help guide you through the thought process.

Also keep in mind, that while you may embark on education for a specific career, it doesn't mean you will work in that field throughout your life. I actually worked in three different fields over the years. However, you have to start somewhere, and you will naturally have some idea of what it is you would like to do.

Today, high school guidance departments and libraries should have the *Occupational Outlook Handbook* on-hand. According to Marianne Finn, counselor and college advisor at Clara Barton High School in Brooklyn, New York, the *Occupational Outlook Handbook* is the bible of career-guidance.

Within this book is every career imaginable with specific requirements, necessary schooling, and other important information relating to the particular career. In addition, check out *www.collegeboard.com* which provides very good career-based information and information on colleges. More resources are listed in the *Suggested Reading and Resources* Section at the end of the book.

I'm thinking about macro-economics as a career. I am interested in business and in dealings with other countries. I also know that there are a lot of job opportunities in economics.

Daniel Ganbeg, High School Student

If you have thought about your career, it is time that you begin to confirm whether your work goal is right for you, is achievable, and will make you happy and able to support yourself. If after researching your chosen career, you feel you are on the right path, it is time to test that.

One of the ways you can do that is to spend some time speaking with an individual who is in the position you would like to hold. If you don't know anyone personally who is in that career, your teachers or guidance counselor can be a resource.

You can also contact a company or facility related to your career interest. The public relations department or human resources personnel can assist you in finding someone in the company who is willing to discuss your interest. Individuals in the workplace are usually delighted to give guidance, and it is a great experience for you to begin to assert yourself, and get firsthand information about your career interest.

In addition to the above, many schools offer cooperative or internship programs in which you can work part-time in your chosen field while you complete your studies. Another important way to affirm your career choice is through volunteer service. I will go into this more deeply later in the chapter.

I cannot say enough about the importance of volunteer service for young adults. Not only does volunteering open the work world to you, but you also contribute greatly to society by assisting those in the workplace to achieve their goals.

SETTING REALISTIC GOALS FOR THE FUTURE

There are various ways in which students choose their careers, and the choices can happen at different points during their high school or college studies.

Some of you reading this will already have chosen your future career. Others may not be so sure at this point. Still others may have chosen their careers, but the career choices may change for some of them as they go through college and their early years of work.

Even if you have a clear idea of what you want to do in your future, it is important that you carefully investigate your interest, making sure this career choice is realistic for you. I will tell you why.

You may recall from my brief history in *Looking Back...* that I was deciding on a career when I was in my junior year of high school. What I didn't say in that brief history was how I arrived at my decision. In the first few years of high school, I knew I wanted a career that involved working with people.

Although I thought about it briefly, I knew nursing would not be for me, as I have always had a queasy stomach when around people that were very ill or bleeding. I then thought about psychology, since, believe it or not, I liked listening to people's problems. This would enable me to work directly with people, but would not involve blood and guts.

At the same time, however, I loved learning languages, particularly French, and thought about being an interpreter. I had a dream of working at the United Nations.

The French language, which at the time was *the international language*, was used very much (Today, English is considered the international language). During the summer between my junior and senior years, I had the opportunity to go on a class trip to

France to study French at a lycée (French high school); however, even while I was in France, I began to realize that although I loved to study languages, I was having difficulty becoming fluent.

I really did not have a talent for languages. Heading into my senior year, I knew that the right place for me was in the field of psychology. As you know, I did not formally use my counseling skills over the years; however, my work in the corporate world, as well as my work in health care, brought me into contact with people. I have been able to leverage my people skills in every job I have had.

This experience illustrates a very important element in thinking about your future career. It is not enough to have a dream of what you want to do in the future.

It is also important that the goal you set is appropriate for your personality and intellect. It is easy to jump at some goal or ideal that looks interesting, but each career has a unique set of requirements.

As an example, you might be interested in the medical field and have a dream of becoming a doctor. You must, however, have a certain level of skill, ability, and commitment for the rigors of medical school and residency.

If you are interested in medicine, but feel you can't reach the goal of becoming a physician, there are many other careers within the medical field that you can pursue. Becoming a nurse (male or female), physician's assistant, paramedic, physical therapist, X-ray or nuclear medicine technician, social worker, administrator of a hospital or nursing home, and many other medical careers can be very rewarding.

Neglecting to do research about what it takes to be in a particular position can lead to great disappointment and disillusionment. Therefore, whatever your interests are today, it is very important that you thoroughly explore those interests, together with your abilities, and all that makes up your whole person.

DEALING WITH UNCERTAINTY ABOUT A CAREER

If high school students don't know what they want to do right away, they should look at what comes naturally to them. They should look at what they like to do, and what they are good at.

Melba Mathurin, Former Model and
Master's Student in Thanatology

It is not unusual for young teens to be uncertain about what they want to do in life. In fact, some high school graduates go on to college without a clear sense of their ultimate goal; however, as I mentioned earlier in the chapter, it is very important that you begin to think about your interests and abilities so that you can begin the process of identifying the most appropriate career for you.

One of the ways you can begin this exploration is to think about what subjects you excel in. Perhaps you do well in math, and love math. You may wonder, *what can I do with a love of math?*

Actually, there are many excellent careers for students who excel in math and who love numbers. Accountants, financial analysts, engineers, stock traders, meteorologists, math teachers, to name just a few, are some of the careers that derive from being good in math.

> *I didn't really know what career I wanted,*
> *but I was interested in computer science and was good in computers.*
> *I decided I would pursue a degree in computer engineering.*
> *I then changed my major before I entered college.*

> *Joseph Glomka*, Color Scientist
> working in film industry

What if you are on the opposite end of the spectrum and like subjects related to English, social studies, or history? Once again, the careers may not seem obvious, but there are many.

Of course, you can always teach these subjects. Teaching has a wide range of specialties in and of itself. You can teach elementary school, intermediate school, high school, or at the college level. With English as a major in college, you can embark on a career in journalism.

Also, *think out of the box.* Do research on jobs needing people. For example, currently there is a shortage of nurses throughout the United States. Nursing is an honorable career that pays well and includes promotional opportunities. It may be hard on your feet, but you would have a great feeling of satisfaction in this type of work.

If you are in junior or senior year of high school and plan on going to college, and you have gone through the process of investigating your interests, and you still don't know what you want to do, there is no need to panic. You should continue to engage in a dialogue with yourself and with others to try to discover your career.

Joe Slomka didn't really know what career he wanted as he prepared to go to college; however, he was interested in computer work, and felt he was skilled at using computers. He decided to major in computer engineering.

Just before he entered freshman year at the Rochester Institute of Technology, he realized that a career in computer engineering might not provide him the opportunity to interface with a lot of people. He pictured computer engineering as being in an inside room, working on the guts of a computer, without much interaction with people on a day-to-day basis.

Since he liked working with people, he changed his major to information technology. After he graduated from RIT, the first job Joe obtained required learning about color science. Since Joe was considered a valuable employee, the firm paid for his master's degree in color science.

Irene Santiago, a client associate at Merrill Lynch & Co., spoke to me about how she hadn't known what she wanted to do even when she was in college. She had decided to major in business, since she knew that this field would encompass various careers. After graduating with a BS in business, and doing an internship, Irene secured the client associate position.

These stories illustrate how your career can be chosen at various points during your teenage years, and how they can be reframed if necessary. Therefore, even though you may not know exactly what your career should be as you enter college, you should choose a major that is closest to your area of interest, as did

Joe and Irene. As you go through your first two years of college, your skills, abilities, and interests should become clearer. Depending on the institution, majors can be changed within the first two years of college, and an internship or work experience can bring your future career into better focus.

> *I wasn't very good in school, but I liked to work with my hands.*
> *I wanted a physical job, and wanted to work hard.*
> *I wanted to do the very best job I could do.*

Robert Tutrone, Owner, CR Landscaping

If you do not plan to go to college, you need to be much more active in thinking about your career. Once again, you need to think about what subjects you like in school, and those in which you excel. Also, think about your interests.

Robert Tutrone never went to college. He told me that he really did not do well in school; however, he had always liked to work with his hands. During and after high school, he worked for a construction company, and then for a landscaper.

He very much enjoyed the landscaping job, and as time went on, he thought he could try to run his own business. He started with a few clients, and now he owns CR Landscaping, Inc. based in Mount Pocono, Pennsylvania.

He has a landscaping and construction crew that does landscaping in the summer, snow removal in the winter, and excavations for new developments. He has several major commercial contracts. Robert attributes his success to ambition, hard work, paying attention to the job at hand, and doing the best job every time.

Once again, if you are having a hard time deciding what you are going to do after high school, and you are not going to college, you must begin now to investigate your likes and dislikes, your strengths and weaknesses. It is also very important to speak to your guidance counselor, if you haven't already, about opportunities for high school grads.

WHAT IS SUCCESS?

I'm having a great life. I love to go to the shop.
Believe it or not, I love Monday mornings.

Robert Tutrone, Owner, CR Landscaping

It's a good time now to talk about the meaning of success. Because so much of your thinking about careers is going to be linked with your goal of being a success, it is important to look at what success really means.

For most people, a successful person is one who has a high-level job and makes a lot of money. Yes, that is one explanation of success; however, it is not the only definition, nor is it the final definition, of success.

Ultimately, you are successful when you are in a job that you like very much, where you feel productive, and where you are making enough money to feel comfortable. If you make a lot of money and are a CEO of a major company, but don't really like what you do, and are not very happy, you may be successful in the eyes of others, but you will not be fulfilled.

If you saw Robert Tutrone on an average day, with his clothes covered in dirt, you might not think he was very successful; however, he is content, loves his work, and has made enough money for his family to move into a larger house with more land. Robert takes several vacations a year, and is able to provide for the education of his three sons.

In today's world, success seems to be wrapped up with the accumulation of a lot of money. While there is nothing wrong with making a lot of money, there is a whole part of life that, as the old saying goes, money cannot buy. There is contentment, the love of work, having time for family and friends, and contributing to society at large.

Success is more than just self-interest.
One must look at what is meaningful in life as a whole.

Christopher Smith, Business Manager, Oratory Church of St. Boniface, Brooklyn, New York

Christopher Smith, who just retired as a business manager in a large Catholic church in Brooklyn, believes you cannot be fulfilled unless you look beyond yourself in your work. An example of what Chris is talking about is evident in the extraordinary experience of Melba Mathurin.

When I spoke with her several years ago, Melba was a thirty-two-year-old former model from St. Croix, Virgin Islands. At the age of eighteen, when she was contemplating college and wanted to pursue a career in psychology, Melba was approached by a scout from the Ford Modeling Agency.

This is every girl's dream, but Melba had some misgivings, since she wanted a college education; however, knowing it was a great opportunity, and with the support of her parents, she accepted the modeling position.

She went to New York and modeled for seven years. Melba admitted it was a life of glamour and travel, but after doing it for five or six years, Melba began to feel unhappy. She began to feel that what she was doing did not have a lot of meaning. She didn't feel fulfilled. She was beginning to think of going back to school.

At the age of twenty-five, she left modeling behind and pursued her degree in psychology. She has worked as a counselor and patient representative, and she pursued a master's degree in thanatology, the study of death and dying. Melba was planning to do her internship in a hospice.

I was very successful as a model, but by around the fifth or sixth year of modeling I was not very happy. I didn't feel fulfilled. It was a hard decision, but I returned to school.

Melba Mathurin, Thanatology Master's Student

The suggestion here is not to put down money or fame. There are many "successful" people who have it all. I wish you could be successful and have all that you want. It is important, however, to keep your perspective on what adds up to success, and know that you will be successful even if you have what some would call a modest job.

If you are ultimately happy, feel fulfilled, are able to support yourself and your family, and have those things in life that you cherish, you *are* a success.

BEGINNING TO MOVE AHEAD—THE STEPS YOU HAVE TO TAKE

You need to take a more active role in what you want to do in life.
Be proactive.

Dennis Straub, former 12th grade Physics Teacher,
Current Aeronautical Engineer

After you have decided on a career, you have done your research, and you fully understand what it will take to reach your goal, it is time to move ahead and begin the process of affirming that goal. It is time to talk to as many people as you can who may be currently in your chosen career field. If possible, it is time to try to obtain a part-time or summer job that has something to do with your career.

Some good ways to explore a future career are: (1) obtain a

volunteer assignment in the field of your interest, (2) obtain an internship, (3) take part in a co-op program while in school, or (4) obtain a part-time or summer job in your chosen career.

Some careers might lend themselves more to practice in a volunteer setting. Others you are anticipating might require that you do some type of internship or work for school credit in a company.

Your teachers and the guidance department in your high school should have information on co-op programs, internships, and volunteer opportunities. In Chapter Four, I will discuss how to approach the search for your first volunteer or paid position.

THE IMPORTANCE OF VOLUNTEER SERVICE

I cannot say enough about volunteer service as a means to develop your work skills and your entire person for the paid workplace.

Giving of yourself in volunteer/community service has four very important results: (1) You learn about the workplace, (2) you have the opportunity to develop and refine your work skills, (3) you might have the opportunity to apply for a full- or part-time position in the same institution, and last, but certainly not least, (4) you make an important contribution to your community through this service. Ideally, you should seek a volunteer assignment in your field of interest.

If you are interested in pursuing a career in medicine, there are numerous opportunities for volunteers in hospitals or nursing facilities.

When I left Merrill Lynch in 2002 and wanted to pursue a career in the medical field, I first obtained a volunteer position in a local hospital. I learned what it means to work in a hospital. I learned what I was best at, and what I liked and did not like. I applied for my first health-related paid position in that same hospital nine months into my volunteer service, and I was offered the job.

I was thinking about pre-med, but didn't like chemistry. I chose to volunteer in a hospital just to reassure myself that I wouldn't be missing out on something I wished I was doing.

Amanda Lee, 17, Volunteer

As much as volunteer service can help you affirm what your career should be, it can also help eliminate a field that would not be appropriate. When I spoke with Amanda Lee, she was a seventeen- year-old hospital volunteer.

Amanda purposely decided on volunteering in a hospital because she had a medical career in mind, but did not feel that working in a hospital was for her. In fact, Amanda stated that her hospital volunteer service reinforced her feeling that she did not like hospital work. She is now thinking about a career in forensic psychology.

Don't always go for the money. It is great to get a chance to work in an internship program or volunteer.

Jamillia Charles, High School Senior and Hospital Volunteer; Career Interest: Physician Assistant

If you are interested in business, there may be less opportunity for day-to-day volunteer service in institutions; however, you can always offer your services on a special project.

Contacting a business employer and offering your services free of charge shows that you are proactive, willing to learn, and want to make a difference. It makes you stand out. You might even be offered pay, even though you offer to work for free! It happened to one of my colleagues and was a great surprise.

What if you don't have an opportunity to work or volunteer in the field of your choice? In this situation, there is a great deal to be gained from doing some type of community service. Even if your community service work does not have much to do with your ultimate work interest, the experience you will gain from working with others in a work environment is invaluable.

When you are doing volunteer/community service work, you are, in fact, working. You need to bring the same workplace skills and your full personhood to the volunteer setting as you would to a paid position.

You have responsibilities. You are in a position to learn. You are accountable for a particular job. You will have a manager, co-workers, and a specific job to do. You must be on time and work a certain number of hours a day, or certain days of the week.

People will depend on you. You will have experience to put on your resume. You will learn a lot of things and come away from the volunteer experience a richer person. In Chapter Five, I will discuss workplace behavior that will be important for both paid and unpaid jobs.

When you are in the workplace, whether as a paid person or

as a volunteer, the same behaviors apply, and will affect how successful you will be in each work venture.

Choosing a career is one of the most important things you will do in your life. Thoroughly researching your interests, and looking at yourself and your personhood in relation to that interest, is critical in leading you to the right path for your success and happiness.

Today, lines are blurred between jobs for men and jobs for women. Women are firefighters, engineers, and workers in the construction field. Men are nurse practitioners. For a well-prepared, hardworking young man or woman, there are wonderful opportunities available. However, in today's economy it may be a challenge to identify and be accepted into the job of your choice.

That is why it is so important how you prepare your person, how you study, how you research your interests and ultimately choose your career, as well as how you will approach an employer and interview for a job.

REFLECTIONS

If you feel certain about your career path, what steps have you taken to thoroughly investigate it?

_____

_____

_____

Based on your investigations into your chosen career, are there any concerns you have? If so, what are they?

_____

_____

_____

If you do not yet know your career path, list some of your interests, your skills, and some of your personality traits. Can you see any potential career coming from this list?

_____

_____

_____

If you are not going to college, have you decided on a trade school, or have you taken steps to set up work after high school?

_____

_____

_____

If you are a junior or senior in high school, and have problems deciding what you want to do in the future, have you discussed this with any professional in school? If not, list the steps you will take to discuss this with your family and professionals at school.

_____

_____

_____

4
—

Searching for Your First Volunteer
or Paid Position

Your first job or volunteer experience is like spring training in baseball.
It's great practice for the big time.

Joseph De Vierno, Managing Director, Audit Practices,
JP Morgan/Chase

If you focus your energies on getting that first job or that big job of your dreams in the future, you will achieve your goal. As long as your goal is compatible with your skills, your life can become all that you dream.

We all have to start somewhere, and you are at the starting gate of your future life—your future career. As Joe DeVierno states at the opening of this chapter, this is your spring training time. When you are working at a part-time or summer job, or volunteering in an organization, you are on the playing field in the position of trainee for the big game to come.

Depending on your age and circumstances you might have already worked or volunteered, or you might have had some experience searching for work. Even if you have already worked, there is still a lot to learn.

Even an experienced worker learns new things every day on the job, and improves in the job search each time he or she moves to another job. As with anything in life, no matter how old you are, you need to continue to research and experience in order to grow.

If you have not as yet worked or volunteered, it's time to prepare for that first experience. The question you may ask is: *How do I begin?*

Looking for work actually is a type of job. It requires learning, judgment, persistence, time for research, and the all-important preparation of your *presence* that we discussed in Chapter One.

The first step you need to consider, whether or not you have already held a job, is how to begin the search. If you are as I was in my teens, and don't have any *connections* to get a job, then you have some work to do.

I was from a working-class family. My father was a carpenter, and others in my family were printers or other blue-collar workers. None of my relatives had ever gone to college up to the point when I graduated from high school. Therefore, I had to start from scratch; however, even though I found the task of searching for work challenging, it was not overwhelming. It was actually kind of exciting.

The important thing is for you to consider the job search a challenge, a part of the job game, and not a chore. In fact, the job search can be very rewarding in terms of experience.

BEGINNING THE SEARCH

The first step in looking for work is deciding what you want to do. If you have a clear idea of your career goal, the ideal work or volunteer experience would be doing something that is related to your field of interest.

If you are not certain what you want to do in the future, your job search can be broader, but it would be a good idea to keep your search within the realm of what interests you. For example, if you think you might be interested in pursuing a career in computer science, try looking for a job that will utilize your computer skills and give you the opportunity to learn more along the way.

Also, keep in mind the unique skills you may have. For example, if you are fluent in a language other than English, there may be many opportunities for you where interpreter services are needed.

It's important to be socially active in school. That's the way you can network and find opportunities for work.

William Hoyt, Embedded Software Engineer Associate, Lockheed Martin

Once you know the type of job you want, then begin the search in earnest. The following are guidelines for the search, both for your search now and for that big job search of the future.

ACCESS THE INTERNET

The internet is the main place most people search for jobs today. You can search for part-time or summer jobs. A number of listings should come up, and you can follow the instructions for applying for a job online.

The end of this chapter will provide sample resumes and cover letters for your reference. Many Internet job sites require you to complete an online application, and/or attach a cover letter and resume.

Also, in the reference section at the end of the book, I list a number of Job Boards that are the most popular and active, and where you should list your resume.

Most job boards will also ask you to set up *alerts* so that you can list categories of jobs that you would want to know about in your area. They also have mobile apps that you can download and then receive the alerts on your smartphone.

FIND A LIST OF EMPLOYMENT AGENCIES

In addition to finding companies or organizations with job openings, you can find employment agencies on the internet.

Some will be local to your home town, and others could

be nationwide. There are both temporary and permanent employment agencies, and you can contact those agencies that have positions near your home.

When you make the call to the agency, you should speak to the person answering the phone like this:

Good morning / afternoon. My name is _____. I am a high-school student (junior, senior, etc.) who is looking for a part-time / summer position. I have skills in _____, _____, and _____ (mention computer, math, writing, etc.). I would like to meet with someone in your agency to discuss opportunities.

Remember what we discussed in Chapters One and Two about communication skills? It's not only important what you say, but how you say it.

Be sure you project your voice when you are on the phone. Be polite, but sound firm and confident. You may not get an appointment after your call, but will be asked to send a resume. Each agency may work differently.

If an agency requests that you e-mail a resume, you will need to write an appropriate cover letter in the e-mail. You can use this opportunity to write some of the same information as noted above:

Dear Recruiter. My name is _____. I am a high-school student (junior, senior, etc.) who is looking for a part-time / summer position. I have skills in _____, _____, and _____ (mention computer, math, writing, etc.). I am interested in discussing available opportunities considering my skills.

I have attached my resume for your review.
I look forward to hearing from you.
Sincerely,
Name
Phone number

I will provide further cover letter samples at the end of this chapter.

LOOK IN LOCAL AND REGIONAL NEWSPAPERS

Become familiar with the employment opportunities section of newspapers, especially local papers. This applies whether you are looking for summer work or for part-time work year-round. Look for entry-level positions in the category of work that interests you.

For example, if you want to work in a large corporation, you can look for positions such as *administrative assistant, clerical, receptionist, data input*, etc.

If you're interested in a sales job, look under *sales* or *retail*. Since you are still in school, you might find a more relevant position for your age and experience if you look in the *Part-Time, Temps*, or *Summer Help* categories.

TALK TO YOUR SCHOOL GUIDANCE COUNSELOR

They will generally have a good idea about potential part-time and summer jobs or volunteer opportunities in your area. The guidance counselor will also be able to advise you on how to approach these opportunities.

BEGIN TO NETWORK THROUGH YOUR FRIENDS, FAMILY, TEACHERS, AND OTHER ACQUAINTANCES

William Hoyt, Dennis Straub, and I all found work through networking at some point. Networking means talking to friends about what they are doing, and asking if they know someone who is hiring.

Networking means joining clubs, and/or attending events where you can meet new people and find out about them and where they may be working. Networking is one of the major ways people find jobs.

When I worked at Merrill Lynch, I was hired first through an employment agency. When I wanted to move on to another department or division, I moved into new positions through my networking efforts.

I moved from being a business manager on the business side to a similar position in technology and then corporate audit. I moved around by contacting managers I had met over the years and discussing opportunities in their departments.

CONTACTING EMPLOYERS

Once you have found some open positions that you would like to apply for, there are several ways you can approach employers, depending on the type of business.

You can: (1) send a resume and cover letter to their human resources department or the hiring manager, (2) make a direct phone call to the hiring manager or human resources, or (3) make contact by phone and send a resume and cover letter.

If an open position is listed in the newspaper, on the internet, or made known to you through your guidance counselor, follow the instructions of the contact on how to apply.

If you want to work in a particular company, facility, or store, but you don't know of any specific job openings, you can make contact by either sending a resume and cover letter, or contacting the employer directly by phone. A phone contact is most appropriate when you are contacting smaller companies or stores.

For example, if you want to work in your local pharmacy, or a nearby Wal-Mart, you might want to make a phone call first to find out if these businesses are hiring.

You would also call an employer if you find a position listed in the newspaper that requests that you make contact by phone. Before making the call, prepare yourself ahead of time. Write down how you will introduce yourself, and make a list of those special skills you have that will qualify you for the job.

In larger businesses, there are two ways you can approach the employer. You can first contact the human resources department and ask if the company hires part-time or summer help, and then ask how you can apply for a position.

On the other hand, if the company or institution is large enough to have different departments, and you are interested in working in one of those departments, you can contact a department manager directly.

For example, maybe you don't know if a particular company or institution is hiring, but you are very interested in gaining experience in a particular field or department.

In this case, you can call the company and find out the name of the person who heads the department you are interested in. You can send that person a resume with a cover letter, describing your interest and what you can bring to the job.

You can then follow-up that resume with a call after about ten days to find out if you are being considered for a job. Later in this chapter you will find a sample cover letter and resume of an individual who is applying for a marketing position with The Gap. The fictional John Smith is sending his resume and cover letter to the marketing manager, since he is interested in gaining experience in that field.

Prior to sending your resume and cover letter to a department manager, you can also attempt a phone contact with the manager to introduce yourself.

When I left Merrill Lynch and wanted to pursue my interest in the health care field, I first contacted the hospital's human resources department about my interest in a concierge position I had seen listed on their website.

When I didn't hear from human resources, I found the name of the hospitality manager and called him directly. I left a message on his voice mail, saying that I had just left the financial services field after many years of service, and was interested in pursuing a career in health care.

I told him I was a business manager with good organizational skills, and if there was a position open, I would like to speak with him. The manager called me within two days, and we set up an interview time. I brought my resume and we discussed it, and he hired me.

You will not always be able to talk to a hiring manager as I did. You might reach a secretary or assistant in many companies. If you do reach a secretary or assistant, politely confirm the name of the manager and obtain his or her title.

Confirm the department name, the correct address, and floor number, and confirm the city and zip code. You can tell the secretary or assistant that you will be sending the manager a resume for his or her consideration. You may also ask for the manager's e-mail address, if you wish to send the resume via e-mail, if they agree to share the e-mail address.

When inquiring about volunteer service, you should make direct contact with a human resources department or department manager; it is a very effective way to obtain a volunteer position. In many cases a company or institution may not have used volunteers in the past, but your call could prompt them to take advantage of your offer of service.

Before you contact an employer by phone, including contacts with human resources personnel, always be prepared with what you are going to say. It may help to write down your thoughts before you make the call. When you speak to the person who answers the phone, speak confidently and with a strong but polite voice.

The example I gave when contacting an employment agency is a good way to start. Be very polite, but confident, saying "Good morning," or "Good afternoon." Next, give your full name. Then, state the reason you are calling.

After you explain that you are inquiring about part-time, summer, or volunteer opportunities, depending on what applies to you, state some special quality that you have that might interest the employer. Make this last statement short, but powerful.

Here's an example:

Good morning. My name is _____. I am calling to inquire about any part-time (summer, volunteer) opportunities in your company (department, facility).

> I am a junior in high school with very good writing and computer skills, and I am interested in working in your company. If it can be arranged, I would like to meet with someone to discuss my background.

At this point, you may be told to hold on while someone else comes to the phone. In this case, repeat everything again. If you are told that there are no opportunities right now, you can ask if you might be able to send a resume to them for future reference.

If the person says, "Yes," ask for the complete name of the person you should send it to, and confirm the physical address as well as the individual's e-mail address. Thank the person you spoke with for his or her time and consideration.

The important thing is to always answer a future employer honestly about your available time and job skills. The more honest and flexible you are, the more respect you will win.

If an employer is interested in you, he or she may ask you specific questions. For example, you may be asked if you can do a particular type of work, or how many days a week you can work.

The important thing here is to answer honestly. Don't commit to more time than you can give, or say you have a skill that you don't. If you are hired and cannot do the job, or cannot meet the job obligations, you certainly cannot expect a good reference from that workplace in the future, and references are all-important as you move from one job to another.

If you don't have a particular skill that the job requires, you can say that you are a quick learner (if you are), and that you are very willing to learn and would like them to consider training you for that skill.

The more honest and flexible you are, the more respect you will win from the potential employer. An employer is likely to take a chance hiring an individual who may not have all of the experience, but who communicates in an honest way, is willing to work hard, and is flexible.

As I will discuss in the next chapter, flexibility is one of the most important things you need to exhibit on the job.

CREATING YOUR FIRST RESUME AND COVER LETTER

You should prepare your resume and cover letter as you begin your search for a paid or volunteer job. Even if you will not work for pay, it is good practice to have your experience, skills, and work objectives outlined on a resume. Remember Ms. Jones in Chapter One.

Ms. Jones did not bring a resume to the interview. As a result, I had no frame of reference from which to ask the most appropriate questions. Preparing a resume helps you to organize your thoughts, your experiences, and your skills.

Your resume provides a window to your whole person, and it gives the interviewer the tool he or she needs to conduct an appropriate interview. When you send a resume, you should also include a formal cover letter—it gives you the opportunity to introduce yourself and your skills to the employer.

Even if you eventually fill out a job application, when you prepare a brief resume and cover letter, it lets the employer know that you are professional and prepared.

You can adjust your resume to reflect or emphasize the skills you have that are required for a particular job. If you are sending your resume to several similar organizations, you can send them the same resume. However, if you are sending your resume to different types of organizations, you may need to change some of the contents of the resume to fit that position.

As a recruiter, I have seen candidates who will send a resume that does not appear to be a fit for the position. When I actually speak with the candidate, they may provide more information that may make them a fit. Not including relevant information to the job on your resume can disqualify you from a position, when in fact, you may have the necessary skills.

The same is true of your cover letter. You should adjust your cover letter to fit the position you are applying for. You can have a basic cover letter, but it is important to change some of the contents to match the position.

I cannot stress enough that *employers look for keywords related to the job in your resume and/or cover letter.*

When sending a resume, you should emphasize those skills you possess that may match the skills needed in a particular institution. In other words, you should keep a common format to your resume, but understand that you can adjust it based on where it is being sent.

If you find five jobs that interest you, send out a cover letter or resume for each job at the same time. (Once again, it can be the exact same resume for each job, or you can adjust the resume accordingly).

Don't wait for each workplace to get back to you before you send out another resume. Don't be afraid to make a call to follow up on your resume if you do not hear from the company or institution.

Generally, I would call if I did not hear from a company within ten days. You can simply call the individual to whom you sent the resume and ask if it was received, and when you might be notified if there is interest in interviewing you.

The resume and cover letter are extremely important in helping you obtain a job interview. Your chances of obtaining an interview for most jobs depends chiefly on how well you communicate your experience and abilities both verbally and in writing.

As we discussed above, your ability to make a good first impression by articulating your interest to a future employer on the phone is one critical factor. This skill will also carry over to the interview. In addition, providing a written synopsis of your experience and skills through a resume and cover letter is essential.

You may wonder what you can put on a resume if you have never worked. Don't forget—you gain skills and experience every day of your life. Skills and experience are gained through school, but can also be gained from your involvement in outside activities. Later in this chapter, I have provided sample resumes for your use. One resume is for students who do not yet have work experience, and the other is for students with some work or volunteer experience.

THE RESUME FORMAT

The major elements you need to put on a resume, in order, are the following: (1) your personal information, (2) your job objective, (3) your education, (4) your work/volunteer experience, and special skills, (5) accomplishments, (6) special awards or organizational memberships, and (7) any outside interests. Specific information under these categories includes the following:

- **Personal Information:** Put your name, address, phone number, and e-mail address, centered at the top of the page.

- **Job Objective:** You can adjust your objective depending on where you are sending the resume, or you can use a generic goal. A generic goal would read as follows: *To obtain a position in which I can enhance my work experience and skills.*

  You can list a specific goal if you wish to impress an employer with your desire to gain further experience in that particular field. For example, if your future career goal is in health care, you can put the following job goal: *To obtain a position in health care that will enhance my knowledge and skills in preparation for my studies in medicine.*

- **Education:** List your education, including your school, your year, and your average (if it is good). For example, list your average if it is B+ or better, especially if it is over 90 percent.

- **Work/Volunteer Experience and Special Skills:** If you have worked or volunteered, list any work or volunteer experience first in this section. List the latest job or volunteer work first. Write a brief paragraph on your job responsibilities, including any promotions, and emphasize any experience that will show your growth or leadership skills on the job.

  If you don't have any work experience, list your special skills, including those classes or subjects in which you particularly excel. Especially, list any social activities in which you might have taken a leadership role. For those who have worked, your special skills and social activities should follow your work experience.

The Work Experience/Special Skills section is the most important part of the resume. You should write this section to impress an employer with your skills, capabilities, and willingness to work and grow.

- **Accomplishments:** Use this opportunity to explain how you might have excelled in a particular activity in school or at work. For example, if you belong to a school or church group, and have completed a successful fund-raising activity as part of that group, explain how you helped this particular effort. Emphasize how you demonstrated leadership qualities.

- **Awards and Memberships:** Even if you haven't worked anywhere yet, you might belong to a youth group at church, or take part in sports or social activities in which you play a particular role. Mention any awards you might have won as part of your role in these activities. You should also mention any organizational memberships. If you don't belong to any organization, or have not received any awards, omit this section.

- **Outside Interests:** This section gives a personal touch to the resume and also helps the employer see your whole person. You can list any number of interests, such as particular sports, reading, music, etc.

Before you finalize your resume read it over carefully. Make sure there are no typos, and that it looks neat to the eye. Also, take a few days to think about everything you have listed. You may have forgotten some things in your first writing.

Maybe you forgot the babysitting job you had last summer, or didn't consider that a job. It is a job, and it should be listed. Maybe you did something special for a family member, such as being a part-time caregiver.

Maybe you helped an elderly man or woman in your

neighborhood by buying groceries or picking up prescriptions. If you are a responsible young adult, you most likely have "worked" in some way.

You should also show your resume to a teacher or guidance counselor before you send it out. They might think of something that could be added, or suggest an adjustment to the resume. Even with my years of experience on the job, I have always reviewed a new resume with a colleague or manager before I sent it out.

If you are going to send a resume to a potential employer, you need to include a cover letter. Your letter should be relatively short, but should include the following main elements:

- A correct name, title, and address of the recipient.

- A brief introduction to yourself and your job goal, and an introduction to your enclosed resume.

- A brief list of your skills that you think make you eligible for the job.

- A closing statement thanking the employer for his or her consideration.

The letter should give the employer a brief picture of you, and should make him or her want to read your resume. It is important that you pay attention to your grammar and make sure it is not too wordy. This letter is an introduction to you and your background.

Once again, the importance of communication skills becomes very evident. If the letter is not written well, it could lessen the chances you will be asked to come in for an interview. It would be helpful if you review the letter with a teacher, guidance counselor, parent, or someone else you would trust to properly critique the letter.

AN IMPORTANT WORD ABOUT SOCIAL MEDIA AND YOUR JOB SEARCH

The use of social media has exploded over the past five or so years, and with it comes the good, the bad, and the ugly. The good is that it is a fast and effective way to communicate, and sites such as LinkedIn or Facebook may be an effective way to find work.

LinkedIn, in particular, is a professional networking site. You can put your profile on LinkedIn for employers to find, and you can also search jobs and find recruiters on LinkedIn.

Facebook and Twitter, as you all know, are the most popular social networking sites. Jobs may be posted on Facebook, and you can post that you are looking for a particular job, and perhaps find recruiters on Facebook as well.

However, you need to be careful about what you post on both your Facebook and Twitter accounts, as well as other social media sites you may use. Many employers now check a candidates' Facebook and Twitter sites to see what they post, as it provides a look into their character.

I have personally had candidates who did not proceed to the interview stage as the employer checked their Facebook accounts and found postings that were racy, belittling, or contained obscenities.

Your Facebook and Twitter accounts are windows to your *person*. So you will want to be careful about what is posted there.

THE INTERVIEW

The important thing is to have an enthusiastic attitude.
Be prepared. This will give you confidence.

Maria Reyes, Financial Analyst

You have sent out resumes, or called some employers, and now you have been asked to come in for an interview. I'm sure you will be excited, especially if it is a job you really want. Even if the job is not your first choice, go on the interview. You should go on as many interviews as possible, for the practice.

Think about your qualities and abilities and
focus on how to communicate them.

Dennis Straub, Aeronautical Engineer

Maybe you have been asked to interview for a volunteer position, and you may wonder how important the interview will be. It doesn't matter whether the interview is for a volunteer or paid position.

The interview is all-important. It means an employer is interested in your background and wants to learn more about you, and decide whether or not you will fit into the environment. This is truly your time to shine.

Believe it or not, I always looked forward to interviews. I viewed them as a challenge. Yes, I was always a little nervous; however, I really looked forward to the interview as a great way to tell the employer what I could do for them—to tell them what I could offer them.

If you view the job interview as you view winning at sports, or achieving something in your favorite social activity, you will do fine. If you like hockey or baseball, you enjoy playing it and you play to win. This is how you have to think of the job interview. You want the job. You think you will enjoy it, and you want to win it.

There are several things you can do to prepare well for the interview. These are not difficult things. They just take a little time and focus.

First, *learn something about the company or institution.* If it is a large company or institution you can search on the Internet and find a great deal of information. You will need to know the basic mission of the company, their clients or patrons, and the type of products they offer. Read about their accomplishments.

Second, *prepare a list of questions* you might ask about the company, the job, and your position within the company.

Third, *think about yourself* and what you can say about your skills and readiness to be a good employee in this job. Most hiring managers will say to you, "Tell me something about yourself."

This will give you an opportunity to discuss yourself in relation to your school, work, and personal life. When you are asked this question, or something like this question, it is time to put your best foot forward in a confident way.

Fourth, *be prepared with a list of your strengths and weaknesses*. When you state your weaknesses, be honest. If the job requires certain computer skills and you are great in some skills, but not in others, state that. You might say, "I am very comfortable with Word and Excel, but I don't know PowerPoint as well; however, I am willing to learn more."

If your weakness is that you may not work particularly fast, and you are concerned that the company wants someone who works quickly, you can say the following: "My strength is that I pay a lot of attention to detail. I want to make sure my work is correct; however, sometimes carefully checking my work may bring the project completion closer to a deadline."

The following could be other examples of your statement of strengths and weaknesses:

My strengths are that I'm well organized and very good at writing and completing projects. I am a quick learner. One of my weaknesses is that I have some computer skills, but need to be more skilled in programs such as Excel and Publisher.

Depending on your particular strengths and weaknesses, you can turn this around, so that maybe you're great in computer skills but don't have particularly good writing skills.

Whatever your strengths and weaknesses are, it is important to give real strengths and real weaknesses. It won't go over if you say that your weakness is that sometimes you work too hard!

Always look professional when you go on a job interview.

Amanda Lee, 17, Volunteer and part-time Worker

After you have prepared for the interview in these four ways, your next step is to dress for the interview. No matter how casual your future employer may allow you to dress once you are hired, you must dress professionally for any interview.

This means a suit, or sports jacket, tie, and pants for young men. For ladies, it means a nice dress, a suit, a skirt with blouse or sweater and blazer, or a pants suit. First impressions mean everything!

As I mentioned in Chapter One, your appearance and your presence are the most immediate way the employer looks at your person.

Once you have dressed for the job, it is time to leave for the job. When you go on your job interview, it is important that you leave early enough to get there on time. Anticipate a lot of traffic, or a slow bus or train, and leave yourself plenty of extra time.

If you are early for the interview, you will have some time to sit and relax and perhaps review in your mind what you have to say. If you arrive in the nick of time, you are likely to feel rushed and hassled, and it may throw you off.

When the interviewer greets you, remember to smile and shake his or her hand firmly. He or she will invite you to sit at a table or in front of his or her desk. You should sit up straight. Then remember what you have to offer.

This is the point when most people, including myself, can get a little nervous or intimidated. This is when you have to remember that you do have skills and that you want to impress this upon the interviewer. Take cues from the interviewer.

Make eye contact. If you are asked a question you cannot

immediately answer, take a few seconds to think it through and give your best answer. Most interviewers will ask you questions that relate to what you put on your resume. They will ask you to expand on what you have stated on your resume, and you should be prepared to do that.

Remember to ask questions when appropriate. You should have a list of questions about the job or company. In addition, if there is something you don't understand or you want clarification on some aspect of the job, do not hesitate to ask the interviewer to explain it further. This shows you are interested and that you are thinking.

I look for enthusiasm, zeal, and spark when I interview a person. If someone is enthusiastic, it will transfer to his or her work.

Terry Rosenfeld, Social Work Manager

Terry Rosenfeld is an experienced social work manager, and had worked in a key position in a major New York City hospital. She states that one of the key issues she has when interviewing social work interns or new social workers for the job, is that some interviewees do not ask questions, or don't ask enough questions. The best interviewees are those who are inquisitive and curious, and this translates into creativity in the workplace. Terry also looks for enthusiasm. Enthusiasm in an interview translates into enthusiasm for the job.

As you are interviewed and get a better feel for the job, you may get the sense that you are not completely qualified for the job; however, if you feel you can learn the job and really want the job, you can state that at the close of the interview.

You might say to the interviewer that you realize you may not have all of the qualifications for the job, but you are very willing to learn. You could say that you are flexible, organized, and very conscientious (hopefully, you are all these things). If you say this with confidence, you may still have a shot at the job.

If your experience and skills seem to be compatible with the job requirements, you can say this to the interviewer. Don't hesitate to express your enthusiasm for the job, and the fact that you will do your very best on the job.

At the conclusion of the interview, always thank the interviewer for his or her time and the opportunity to interview for the job. Once again, shake his or her hand firmly.

After completing the interview, you can add a nice touch by sending the interviewer a brief note formally thanking him or her for the opportunity to interview and for his or her consideration.

Based on the information you learned at the interview regarding the specific job opening, you can state that you feel your skills and experience would make you a good candidate for the job. This note will give you an opportunity to once again express your interest in the position.

What I have mentioned thus far are the necessary preparation, and the basic skills you must bring to a job interview. It would take up a lot of this book to talk about all of the potential questions an interviewer might ask and to mention every possible interview situation. In the *Suggested Reading and Resources* section at the end of the book, I have included resources to help enhance your interview skills.

DEALING WITH REJECTION

It is inevitable that you will not receive an offer for every job you apply and interview for. Sometimes, it might just work out that you will be given a job offer after your very first job interview.

This is great—however, most people can interview for four or five or more jobs before they get an offer. This can be discouraging, but it is part of the job game. When you don't receive a job offer, you shouldn't really look at it as a *rejection* of your person.

Employers will look at several things to determine whether you are the right fit for a particular job. They will look at your presence (which is something you have the most control over), but they must also look at your particular skills. When you are not given a job offer, it is most helpful if you speak to the employer directly.

Politely ask him or her if there was a particular reason that you did not get the job. Hopefully, the employer will answer you honestly and you can grow from there; however, many times you will only receive a form letter informing you that you are not accepted for the job.

In any case, try to examine yourself and look closely at how you did on the job interview. Maybe you will realize that you did not have the particular skills required.

Other times, it may be more difficult to understand; however, you must realize that someone must have come in to interview before you or after you, who either was more skilled, more enthusiastic, or had some particular attribute that made this person more qualified for the job.

Don't get discouraged. Everyone has dealt with job rejection. You must think, examine, adjust, and forge ahead. In addition to your own introspection, you might want to review your interview experience with a parent, a teacher, or a guidance counselor. They might see something that you did or said that you were not aware of.

The more you interview, the more expert you should become. It's like anything else—practice makes perfect. Therefore, persist in your job search until you get that offer.

WHAT JOB OFFER SHOULD YOU ACCEPT?

It's important that you try different work.
You have to take some risks in finding/accepting work.

Rosanna, MS Candidate, Occupational Therapy

If you have gotten one job offer and it is the job of your choice, you probably won't have any question about accepting the offer. The only thing you need to do is to confirm the terms of the offer, the hours and days of the week, and the salary. If it is a volunteer situation, there will be no salary, but you will want to confirm your responsibilities and your work days.

If you receive more than one job offer, and you are torn between the two, you must take some time to weigh the pros and cons of both jobs. Look at factors like job challenge, the people you will be working for and with, the logistics, the salary, and go with your best assessment and your gut feeling.

If you receive one job offer, and are not certain it meets all of your needs, you need to review whether or not you have a chance at receiving another offer. This is where you must keep your expectations in line.

As a young adult you can't expect to make a lot of money and have the job of your dreams right away. If the job offer is not for the job of your choice, you may need to accept that job because of the experience it will bring you.

You must be careful not to reject an offer unless you are certain other offers will be forthcoming. Unless the job is too inconvenient, or you have learned something particularly unattractive about the job, it is important for you to begin somewhere. Rosanna, a Master's student, told me that she worked in several part-time jobs as part of her career research while in college.

Remember that every job I accepted, from the time I came out of college through my second and third careers, was a job for which I was overqualified. Yet, because of my achievements in each job, I was able to move ahead. I took a few steps back to move forward in the right direction.

You should look at every job opportunity as a stepping stone. Gain some experience, and go for more. Gain more experience, and go for the gold. The more you can put on your resume, the more opportunities you will have to ultimately get your job of choice in the future.

As you can see, there is a lot of work to do to get a job, particularly a first job. Once you have done this, however—searched for the job, created the resume, prepared for the interview—it gets easier to master the skill in the future.

As you can see, some of this will be trial and error, particularly the job interview, but it is all a great life experience for you. As I said in the beginning of this chapter, consider the job search a great game in which you have to achieve. Work at it to win, and you will win big.

SAMPLE RESUME 1

Ideal for a student with no work experience

John Smith
100 Spring Street
Schenectady, New York 12305
Home telephone # 518-000-000
E-mail address: jsmith@aol.com

Objective: To gain experience in the field of sales and marketing

Education: Schenectady High School

Expected date of graduation: June 2019, Maintaining 95% average.

Special Skills: Excel in English, Math and Computer Science. Have received exceptional grades in writing and in oral presentations.

Accomplishments:

*   Served as assistant editor of school newspaper for past two years. Suggested to editor that we choose some new student writers to research and write more creative and interesting articles. By changing some of the content of the newspaper, have increased student interest. Some of the new content includes articles that will keep students aware of activities not just in the school, but in the community as well.

*   Assisted in school fund-raising activities. Was included on committee to plan junior year dance and auction that raised almost $2,000.

Awards and Memberships:

*   Member of National Honor Society
*   Received award for excellence in writing for school newspaper.
*   As part of swimming team, won award for last two years in competition with other area schools.

Outside Interests: Enjoy sports such as swimming, basketball, and hiking. Interested in starting my own website.

SAMPLE RESUME 2

Ideal for a student who has some work/volunteer experience

Janet Garcia
100 Beach Drive
Norfolk, Virginia 23509
Home Telephone #:757-000-0000
E-mail address: jgarcia@msn.com

Objective: To obtain a position in a health care facility to broaden my experience in the medical field.

Education: Hampton Bays High School

Expected Graduation: June 2018, Maintaining 92% average.

Work/Volunteer Experience:

Norfolk Community Hospital volunteer
June 2017–September 2017
Assigned to various hospital units to ensure patients received information packets, and assisted patients and families in understanding hospital policies regarding visiting hours. Sometimes assisted patients with feeding at mealtimes, and did errands for nursing staff as requested.

McDonald's part-time
April 2016–December 2016
Worked weekends taking orders at McDonald's.

Special Skills: Excellent in computer programs Word, Excel, and PowerPoint. Have very good communications skills and phone manner. Fluent in Spanish.

Accomplishments: Served as leader of teen church group that read for the poor in winter 2016. We served over 100 low-income families through our efforts.

Awards/Memberships:
- Member of National Honor Society
- Received science award for project related to atmosphere and the greenhouse effect.
- Was named most valuable player in girls' softball team in Spring 2015.

Outside Interests: Enjoy walking and dancing. Write poetry.

SAMPLE COVER LETTER FOR JOHN SMITH

Ideal for a student with no Work/Volunteer Experience

March 30, 2018

Mr. Harold Martin, Manager
Marketing Division
The Gap Stores
3 Main Street
Schenectady, New York 12301

Dear Mr. Martin,

I am writing to express my interest in a part-time or summer opportunity in your marketing division. I am a junior in high school and intend to pursue a major in marketing after I graduate high school in June 2019. I believe it is important that I begin to gain experience in the marketing field, and I am open to any entry-level position in which I can assist your staff.

As you will note on my enclosed resume, I excel in writing and have shown creativity as assistant editor of our school newspaper. I am a hard worker and enjoy project work. I am flexible and organized and would like to bring these skills to the workplace.

I look forward to hearing from you, and thank you for your consideration.

Sincerely,

John Smith

Please note that the letter above does all the following things: (1) States purpose for writing, (2) States current grade at school, (3) States career goal, (4) Admits that this is a first job, (5) Refers to the resume, (6) Refers to accomplishments/leadership qualities exhibited in school or outside activities, (7) States strengths, and, (8) Thanks the recipient of the letter for his/her consideration.

SAMPLE COVER LETTER FOR JANET GARCIA

Ideal for a Student with some Work/Volunteer Experience

March 30, 2018

Ms. Madeline Marks, Manager
Human Resources
Grace Nursing Home
33 Main Street
Norfolk, Virginia 00000

Dear Ms. Marks,

I am writing to express my interest in a summer position at your facility. As you will note on my enclosed resume, I intend to pursue a career in health care. I have already volunteered, last summer, at Norfolk Community Hospital. I would like to continue to gain experience in the health care field, and have been told by my guidance counselor that your facility will be hiring this summer.

I enjoy working with people and had a very good experience working with staff and patients at Norfolk Community Hospital. I am very friendly and have a good phone manner. I enjoy leading a project, and can assist the staff of Grace Nursing Home in organizing social activities for the residents.

I look forward to hearing from you. You can reach me at 000-000-0000, or by e-mail at jgarcia@msn.com.

Thank you for your consideration.

Sincerely,

Janet Garcia

Please note that the letter above does all the following things: 1) Introduces the purpose of the letter, (2) Refers to the resume, (3) Refers to the open position, (4) Gives a short history of experience, (5) States strengths as they would apply to the job, (6) Thanks the recipient for her consideration.

REFLECTIONS

Have you ever made a list of your strengths and weaknesses? If not, please think about yourself and begin listing your strengths and weaknesses.

_____

_____

_____

Have you ever applied for a paid or volunteer job? If so, what steps have you taken to apply?

_____

_____

_____

If you haven't yet applied for work, what steps will you take to apply?

_____

_____

_____

List some of the things that concern you about a job interview.

_____

_____

_____

Based on what you read in this chapter, how do you think you can address your concerns about a job interview?

_____

_____

_____

5
—

Behavior in the Workplace

Being responsible and knowing how to conduct yourself in the workplace is key. This includes dressing appropriately, speaking properly, being courteous to others, and doing your tasks quickly and efficiently.

Leandra Flores, High School Volunteer

You are now on the job and in the game! Everything that went before—preparing your image; gaining skills through school and life experience; succeeding in your job search; and performing well in an interview, all lead here—to the workplace.

As an athlete prepares for the game and then must give his or her best performance, you are now in the real thing, and will be called upon to do your best. If you have done everything right— if you have prepared your whole person for this new phase of your life—you will be in a position to use your innate abilities along with your new-found skills to succeed in the workplace.

Your innate abilities and skills are two essential elements for success in the workplace; however, other tangible and intangible attributes or behaviors are also essential for your success. As a former high school student, Leandra Flores sums up some of the major elements of appropriate workplace behavior: *dress, communication, courtesy, and efficiency.*

You will recall these are the same elements discussed several times throughout the book in terms of developing your whole person. You will now see the importance of these attributes when it comes to finally being on the job. They are the most obvious behaviors in the workplace, and paying attention to them will give you a good head start in making your mark in the workplace.

UNDERSTANDING THE WORK ENVIRONMENT

There are many more workplace behaviors to discuss, but first I want to give you an understanding of the basic work environment. Obviously, different jobs and different places of work will have different environments; however, there are some basics to every work environment.

It may be elementary to say that work environments are made up of people, but people are what makes the work environment tick and what provides the flavor to the work environment. The workplace is like a small world. It is like a family.

In the world and in the family, there are different people with different personalities and styles. This is also true in the workplace.

Your role in the workplace involves not just the tasks you are asked to do. Your role is to be an active participant in a team of individuals who must accomplish a certain task or project.

You will have a specific responsibility in that team, and your performance will affect this team. Everyone else in that team affects the others as well, so that you can have a work dynamic that is either productive or nonproductive.

As a result, part of your responsibility is not just the tasks you are asked to perform, but also the way in which you interact with others: your manager and co-workers.

The workplace is a very interesting place but also sometimes a challenging place. The ideal workplace is one in which a group of people are mature, are respectful of one another, are efficient, and have a good work ethic—that is, the group works in a positive way toward the completion of the workplace goals.

When you first enter the workplace, you will begin to assess the particular environment of that workplace. You will see how different people work. You will see who is friendly and helpful, and who might keep to themselves.

Throughout this book you have learned how to prepare your whole person to get to the workplace and succeed. Now, I will let you in on some other secrets to help you through your first work experiences so that you can work most effectively and make a significant contribution.

WORKPLACE BEHAVIORS 101

Professionalism

    Courtesy

        Good Attitude

            Follow-up

                Communication

                    Respect

                        Integrity

                    Dependability

              Efficiency

            Organization

        Flexibility

    S M I L E

THE FIRST DAY AND WEEK ON THE JOB

One of your early jobs may have been working at a summer camp, working in a retail store, or getting a volunteer position or internship in a place related to your future career.

The first day on the job is always a little unsettling. I always looked forward to my first day on the job with a combination of hope and anxiety. I hoped it would be a great experience, but I was also concerned about whom I would meet, how I would get along with my manager, and how well I would perform those first tasks. Once the first day passed, I usually was able to relax a little.

Most people approach their first day of work with many of the same feelings. It is a new world you are entering, and as with any new experience, there is a fear of the unknown. Just as we have discussed throughout this book, the more you prepare your whole person for this new experience, the more confident you will be and the better you will do.

Depending on where you will work, before you even start on the job you may receive information from a human resources department or manager regarding your schedule, ID card, benefits, sick time, or time off for vacation.

If you do receive this type of information, or any reading material about your workplace, make sure you read this information and understand it before you start on the job.

Take the necessary time to complete a task accurately. Check your work thoroughly, and don't be afraid to ask questions!

Mary Johnson, former Owner/Manager,
Corporate Events Group

When preparing for your first day of work, think about how you prepared for the interview. Before you interviewed for this job you should have learned something about the company or facility.

You should have dressed appropriately. You should have been on time, and carried yourself with confidence and with a smile. This is how you should approach your first day of work. Remember that you have something to offer the employer.

When you arrive at work, your manager or a designee will probably meet with you initially to introduce you to others and show you how the office or department or facility works. You will probably not remember everyone's name at first. That's okay—nobody does.

Your manager, or someone he or she designates, will either give you an orientation to the job or have you immediately begin a task. Remember to ask questions if you don't understand a task. Remember that no question is stupid, especially when you are new at a job.

Be aware that your manager and co-workers will also cut you some slack during the first day or week you work, knowing that it may take longer for you to complete a task; however, your responsibility is to complete whatever tasks you are given in a timely and efficient manner.

Remember the importance of checking your work. It is far better to take a few minutes more to complete a task than to hand in something containing mistakes. According to Mary Johnson, the former owner of The Corporate Events Group, *check and recheck* is a good motto for job security!

In managing an event planning business, Mary Johnson had a lot of experience hiring first-time employees for special event positions. Mary states that many of these young employees were very bright, quick, and enthusiastic; however, as first-time workers just out of school, they were often stuck in "test mode" from their school experience.

Instead of asking questions when they didn't understand the task assigned, they would wing it as they did with exams in school, hoping for a passing grade. There is really no passing grade in the workplace. Things must be done correctly.

In order to encourage her employees to perform their duties most efficiently, Mary had a sign in her office that read, *This Is Not A Test*. This reminded them of the need to perform at their best.

Another important behavior during your first days of work is to take notes. This is particularly important in an office or administrative job. Especially during your first days on the job, you will be learning a lot of important information.

Your manager or another employee may be walking you around the facility and telling you a lot of important information. You will be learning how your particular department or institution or company runs.

You will be learning important contacts, information on how to do certain tasks, perhaps important phone numbers, and many other things. You can't possibly remember everything right away. You must write down certain information and keep it in a handy place. A small notebook will do.

When I was hired as a hospital concierge, I had to learn about the unit and how the unit was run. I started writing down information in a small notebook. I kept that notebook with me and referred to it almost a year later when I was already a supervisor. There was vital information in that notebook that sometimes I had to refer to.

Depending on the type of first job you have, you may be given assignments that are relatively mundane. You may file, make copies, and do messenger work. You may do more professional tasks such as generating reports and using customer service skills, but you may still have to do mundane tasks.

All jobs, no matter how professional, will always include a certain amount of grunt work. You must always get your hands into whatever it is that you need to do. It may not be your favorite task, but your willingness and good attitude toward this type of task are what an employer will notice.

I was a vice president at Merrill Lynch for many years, and yet sometimes I had to send my own faxes, make copies, put books together, answer someone else's phone, or do some other distracting type of work. I just had to do it.

Learn to follow instructions and improvise. Sometimes, in the beginning, I was not sure of what to do, as the floor manager was very busy.

Victor He, High School Volunteer

During those first days of work, you may be given a task and maybe your manager will not be available to answer a question. In this situation you may need to be creative and take initiative.

Victor He had to do this when he was selected as a volunteer. Maybe you will have answered the phone and it is a person who needs to speak to your manager right away, and you don't know where he or she is.

In this case, your judgment is being called to task. You need to try to reach your manager and relay the message. If you don't know how to do this because you are new, you need to improvise.

For example, ask someone else in the office where your manager can be reached. Check your manager's calendar to see if your manager is at a meeting. You need to think and do your best to complete this task.

Never say you don't know where someone is, or you don't know about a particular thing. Rather, you should answer that you will find out where your manager or co-worker is, or that you will try to find an answer to a person's question.

In addition to being helpful to the person who is asking for information, you will learn more about your job and how to navigate through the system.

As you go through your first day, then your first week of work, things will get easier for you. You will have assessed the work environment. Most employees will be very helpful to you, assisting you to learn your way around the system and learn the right way to do things. You will soon become comfortable and that initial feeling of anxiety will begin to fade away.

Always be prepared to be doing something.

Nicole Boles, 17, Volunteer

Remember to always ask for something to do if you have finished a task and no one has given you something else to do. Take the initiative. This is a very important professional standard.

During the first week of work, your active assessment of

the workplace, your efficient completion of tasks, your judgment calls, and your initiative will be especially noted. Also, don't be afraid to ask for something that you think you will need to complete a job.

For example, you might need a personnel list or list of departments to help you contact people, and perhaps your manager or co-workers forgot to give it to you. Don't be afraid to ask for it.

APPLY YOURSELF AND PERSIST

Motivation and effort are the keys.

Ali Hussein, 17, Volunteer

If there is one mantra in this book, it is this: *Apply yourself and persist*. In Chapter Two, I discussed the importance of applying yourself and practicing persistence in your studies.

This is critical in school, and crucial in the workplace. No matter what tasks you are given in any type of work, you can only succeed if you apply yourself and persist.

As volunteer Ali Hussein states, motivation and effort are critical in preparing for work and in the workplace itself. While some of the tasks in a first or second job could be relatively mundane, other assignments may be real challenges to you.

You might be working someplace that is short staffed and you are picking up part of someone else's work. You might have a manager who thinks you are very bright and wants to test your skills while you help him or her complete a very important project.

You may struggle with some projects and need some assistance from others on the job. This is the true test of your skills, your patience, and your professionalism.

It's important in the workplace to be able to ask for the advice of others... there is always something to learn from others.

Rosanna, Candidate for MS, Occupational Therapy

If you are in this type of situation, this is the time to ask as many questions as possible, to review your work on an ongoing basis with your manager, and to find creative solutions to problems.

As Rosanna says, you can always ask the advice of others who have been at the job for a while. You will always learn something from others, and maybe one new bit of information will make all the difference in the world.

If you persist in finding a solution, you will find the way to solve the problem and complete the task successfully. If you apply yourself and persist, you will seek out the information you need to succeed in the project and in the overall workplace.

Remember the importance of organization skills. Organize your work according to priority. If you don't know what task is top priority, ask your manager. Once you know the priorities, you can organize your work appropriately.

If you have a complex task, remember to break it down into parts. As we discussed in Chapter Two, all projects are made up of various parts. If you can first organize those parts in your mind, and then write an outline, you can successfully put together the whole task.

All through my career I was given projects that were challenging, and I wondered how I would ever complete them. I wondered if I could really succeed. When this happened, I took some time to think the whole thing through. Gradually, by thinking it through, organizing the parts and asking questions, I found the way to proceed.

I always felt most rewarded when I finished a project that was particularly challenging. The more you bend your mind and think things through, the more you will develop your problem-solving skills. These skills become increasingly important as you move on to more responsible jobs.

COMMUNICATION AND FOLLOW-THROUGH

Remember to communicate... communicate... communicate. I cannot say it enough! In any type of job, regular communication with your co-workers and your managers is essential. I learned the hard way in my early years of work how important it is to communicate. It was a lesson I will never forget, and it is something I have emphasized with my staff throughout my work experience.

I was twenty-nine years old and in my first administrative position at Merrill Lynch. I was beginning to take on more responsibility, and one of the things I had to coordinate was an important trading room move.

It was the 1980s and Wall Street was booming. Our department was one of several which were moving traders from one part of the trading room to another in order to give them more space to expand. My job was to work closely with the administrative manager of the division, who was managing all of the moves.

By the time the details of the move were finalized, we were nearing the Christmas holiday. The trading manager in my department was very eager to have the move take place. I was following up with the administrative manager in charge of the total project, and I was not able to move our part of the project along very quickly. I kept getting excuses and did not have the expertise at that time to better expedite the moves.

I prepared my part of the project as best as I could, and then the holidays came. I was surprised to receive a call on New Year's Eve from my manager, the department chairman. He mentioned to me that the trading manager had complained to him that I was not moving fast enough to complete this project, and he felt that I was not doing my job.

I was very upset because I had been doing my best, and I outlined to my manager all of the steps I had taken and advised him how many times I had followed up with the administrative manager. Both my manager and the trading manager were not aware of all I had done, because of one simple thing.

I had not communicated to them all of my efforts to date, nor the difficulties I was experiencing in getting our part of the project completed.

At the end of the conversation with my manager, he encouraged me to communicate all of my efforts to the trading manager and to continue to keep him informed. I took his advice. Once I kept our trading manager continually informed, there were no further problems or doubts that I was doing my job.

In addition, by relaying the status of the project, and the difficulties I was having in getting the project off the ground, I enabled the trading manager to discuss the situation with his colleague, and the project began to move. This was a total eye-opener for me.

From then on, no matter what type of work I was assigned throughout my career, I always provided my managers with an ongoing status report so that they knew I was working my best on it.

In addition to communicating with your manager, it is essential that you communicate regularly with your co-workers. It shows your respect for them, and it is proper work protocol to keep your co-workers informed about work issues that you share.

This is especially relevant when you are asked to provide certain information to your co-workers, or if you receive a call from a co-worker requesting certain information.

A professional always returns a phone call, even if it is just to acknowledge that you received the request and will be working on it. It is never professional to ignore phone calls or return calls hours or days later.

When someone calls you and is in need of certain information, or is asking you a question, this person is awaiting a response and it is rude not to respond. It takes a little bit of time to return a phone call, and you gain tremendous respect by communicating regularly with your peers and managers.

Good follow-through is essential. You must not drop the ball; otherwise, you can lose credibility and dependability.

Tracey Lawson, Senior Software Sales Executive

Follow-through on your work is another essential work behavior you must master. It means that in every type of task or project, you should do everything possible to follow all of the necessary steps from start-up to completion.

It means that you don't leave anything half-done because you are waiting for some information. It means that you ask questions and seek information and solutions to complete a project well.

It means that if you are given a project or several projects, it is not enough to ask for information and just wait and wait until you are up against a deadline and cannot come through with the product. You must be proactive in getting what you need.

Follow-through also relates to the issue of communication that I mentioned above. If you are asked to provide certain information, good follow-through means that you will provide that information in a timely manner.

Like good communication, good follow-through means that you are working at your best. Good communication and follow-through help you master your job function and build good work relationships at all levels.

HANDLING CONSTRUCTIVE CRITICISM

Many new employees today cannot take constructive criticism.
They don't see the opportunity for learning and growth.

Terry Rosenfeld. Social Work Manager

Nobody is perfect. No matter how efficient you are on the job, there will be times when your manager will need to critique your work, point out mistakes, make suggestions, or advise a different way of working or approaching a problem.

When we think we have done a good job, and our manager points out something, a common reaction is to be defensive. We want to defend our work, and sometimes cannot see the reason for the criticism.

According to Terry Rosenfeld, this attitude is very prevalent today, and it gets in the way of learning and growth. You must always be open to constructive criticism. Listen to your manager closely.

Even if the mistake or criticism is not immediately obvious or understood, be open to the correction and make the recommended adjustments. In time, the reason for the criticism will usually be obvious.

Remember that there is a lot to learn from managers and peers, and you will never stop learning, even after years in the workplace. This is how you develop and grow into an exemplary employee. Be flexible and patient with others who do not immediately see your way of thinking or doing things.

Remember that there could be several good ways to do a

particular task, and your manager will have a good reason to ask you to complete a task in a particular way.

RESPECT AND BE RESPECTED

Get rid of any attitude you had in high school.
Work is not a place to tolerate attitudes.

Katherine Sanchez, 17, Volunteer

You cannot expect to do well on the job, and to have the cooperation of your peers, your manager, or any clients or patrons unless you respect everyone you work with.

Respect means that you will treat everyone with courtesy no matter how you feel about them. You will not feel warm and fuzzy about everyone you work for or with. As a professional, despite your feelings, you must respect everyone in the workplace and that respect should come back to you.

Katherine Sanchez puts it bluntly when she says to, "get rid of the attitude." Hopefully, as discussed in Chapter One, you will work on your feelings and attitudes and *have it together* before you get to the workplace.

Luz King, an information security analyst at the Federal Reserve Bank, states that a good attitude is one of the most important behaviors in the work place.

A person's attitude affects everyone and everything in the workplace. If there is something about the job that you do not like, or if you feel you are doing more than others, you should not walk around with an attitude. The professional employee speaks with his or her manager about problems in the workplace and should be comfortable to discuss any important issues with his or her manager.

It is crucial for you to develop a positive and accepting attitude in the workplace. Good feelings about yourself and others are critical for appropriate workplace behavior.

Remember the *success equations* from Chapter One? If you have your *whole person* together, you should value yourself and that should help you value others. Valuing others builds relationships. Remember that if you want to be treated as a professional, you need to act as a professional.

If you want respect, you need to respect others. For the most part, everything in the workplace, and in life, is reciprocal. You reap what you sow.

You will gain tremendous respect and support if you treat others with respect, greet them with a smile, and have a can-do attitude about your work.

WORKPLACE ETHICS

Don't bargain with trust. People won't trust you
if you don't have integrity.

Jose Hernandez, Regional Traffic Operations Manager,
Virginia Department of Transportation

There are two types of workplace ethics that are important. One is the basic work ethic. If you have a good work ethic you will do your job to the best of your ability.

You will be reliable. It means you come to work on time, or you call your manager before your work time if you will be unavoidably late or absent.

A good work ethic also means responding in a timely manner to requests, handing in work on time, and treating everyone in the workplace with respect. In summary, a good work ethic means dedication to the job.

Another part of workplace ethics involves trust and integrity. It involves the respect for confidentiality and the discernment of right and wrong. Ethical behavior means that you work with the good of the workplace in mind.

It means that you will not cheat in any way, or look into things that you shouldn't. You are ethical when you are given confidential information and do not leak that information to anyone. You are ethical when you don't carry gossip.

You can be fired faster for one breach of confidence than if you made mistakes on every report you completed. If you have developed your whole person to include basic moral values you will not have to think about behaving in an ethical way. You will be ethical in everything you do.

Jose Hernandez, regional traffic operations manager in Virginia, has said he will not promote an individual who does not have integrity.

The news today abounds with scandals in corporate America.

The scandal at Enron Corporation that dominated the news several years ago was one of the biggest scandals ever in the United States.

Enron was a huge natural gas pipeline company based in Houston, Texas. Over a period of years, its management team wooed investment banking firms into some unusual deals that eventually cost investors millions of dollars.

As a result of its unethical activities, Enron went bankrupt and collapsed. It was a case of not only promoting shady energy deals, but also inflating its profits that caused Enron's eventual crash and huge investor losses.

The actions of one or a few employees can wreak havoc on a company and on the clients it serves. Fortunately, most individuals are trustworthy and honest.

Each workplace has its set of policies and procedures, and it is crucial that you understand these policies and follow the guidelines of the workplace at all times.

You may not think it is a big deal if you peek into someone's personnel file that is on your manager's desk; however, it is a personal document and you betray the confidence of that employee and the workplace.

There is a right and wrong way of behaving, and you can ruin your life, and that of others, if you do not abide by the rules of the workplace.

SOCIALIZING, OFFICE ROMANCES, AND THE OFFICE PARTY

Now we come to the fun stuff. As I mentioned earlier, the workplace is made up of people, and this is what adds so much interest to the workplace. You will form friendships and may even begin socializing away from work with some of your co-workers.

You will also find yourself socializing while on the job, and this is where you need to be aware of the limits. Everyone socializes a bit on the job. Managers will socialize with their staff, as well as co-workers with one another, at different points in the workday.

Some socializing is healthy and it helps reduce workplace stress; however, socializing should never interfere with anyone's work or productivity.

When you are up against a deadline and the workplace is especially hectic, you need to be aware that it is not the time to socialize. Unless the socializing takes place over a lunch hour, it is not usually appropriate to socialize for more than a few minutes. Exceptions to this include special occasions in the workplace.

For example, there may be office celebrations for someone who is getting married, or your manager may encourage a more casual work environment on holiday eves when the workload is particularly light.

As you become familiar with your particular workplace you will come to understand what is acceptable socializing. Remember that your main reason for being at work is to produce a product. Anything that interferes with that could lead to problems for you.

One type of socializing is particularly tricky. It is the office romance. It is not unusual for two individuals at work to be attracted to each other; however, the workplace romance has potential for real problems.

There are occasions when a workplace romance leads to something more. Many such romances do not last and can be a source of discomfort to both parties if the romance falls flat. If you and a co-worker are attracted to each another, you must keep it professional at work.

Tracey Lawson, a senior software sales executive, advises that individuals who are romantically involved should not be seen together often at work. If they want to have lunch with each other, they should not leave together, but should meet somewhere.

There is nothing more volatile for starting the gossip machine than a romantically-involved couple in the workplace.

> *Women can immediately disqualify themselves for a promotion by how they act at the office party.*

Tracey Lawson, Senior Software Sales Executive

Office parties are another way to socialize and can be great fun. For as long as office parties have existed, there has been the potential for workers to make fools of themselves drinking too much or behaving badly.

When you are at an office party you need to remember that you are at an office party, not a friend's party. You can have fun, socialize as much as you want, but you must remember that you are with managers and co-workers.

If you let your hair down too much, you will be the talk of

the office the next day. You could disqualify yourself from a promotion just by the wrong moves at an office party.

WORKPLACE INTERACTIONS AND CONFLICTS

Since the workplace is made up of people with differing backgrounds, ethnicities, feelings, thoughts, and ways of working, workplace interactions can be very interesting. Just like a family, work interactions may also give rise to conflicts. Fortunately, people generally work well with each other because together they have to produce for the company or facility.

In my various jobs with different managers and co-workers, I am happy to say, most of my work experience has been very rewarding with minimal conflict. There has been camaraderie among my peers and I have been well mentored by most managers. You will find this to be true in most of your job experiences.

Sometimes, however, things may not run so smoothly. There could be differing opinions among a team of workers on how to complete a project. There could be some jealousy that comes out in various ways. Your manager could be moody, or maybe the chemistry between you and your manager is not what you would have hoped it would be.

In these situations, you have to learn to cope with a less than ideal situation in a professional way. You need to carefully assess the situation you are in and respond to it maturely. That means you will not resort to confrontation, yelling, swearing, or exhibiting a poor attitude.

If you are having a problem with co-workers, let them know that there are boundaries. Always speak nicely to your co-workers.

Amanda Lee, Volunteer

At the age of seventeen, Amanda Lee had already worked in two part-time jobs and completed volunteer service. Her advice in dealing with problems in the workplace is *bite your tongue*.

When I asked Amanda how she has handled a difficult situation in the workplace she told me that if she feels a co-worker is speaking out of turn or overstepping his or her bounds, she lets them know that there are boundaries. She tells them nicely that she feels that what has been said, or what they are doing, is not appropriate and does not make her feel comfortable.

There are many co-worker and manager issues that can arise in the workplace. If it is an issue with your manager, you can tell your manager in a calm, professional way that you would like to speak to him or her. A manager will generally respect an employee's feelings if approached in this manner and will work with you to solve the problem.

You can do the same with a co-worker. If something is bothering you about the co-worker, ask to speak with him or her privately. Discuss your feelings, and how you think your interaction can improve.

No matter how the co-worker responds, do not lose your professionalism. Usually, if you respond professionally, the co-worker will back down and will be forced to respond to you in a similar way.

Fortunately, real workplace conflicts that could affect your feelings about the job are relatively rare. More common will be your need to exercise patience and understanding when others in the workplace do not work the way you would like them to work, or are not as responsive as you would like them to be to your needs.

You need to exercise this patience and understanding in every part of your life as you deal with people because, as you know from your family and school, everyone is different.

MAKING THE MOST OF ANY POSITION—THE SECRET OF SUCCESS

Young people shouldn't be afraid to explore different opportunities. Everything leads to where your complete person should be.

Melba Mathurin, Former Model/
Candidate for MS, Thanatology

As I mentioned earlier in this chapter, your first job or two might involve relatively mundane tasks, or you might have a position that is somewhat challenging.

Whatever your circumstances, a new job will always bring the opportunity for new learning and meeting new people who could influence and mentor you for the future job of your dreams. You need to recognize that in every work situation, even if it's just flipping hamburgers or handing out fudge at the New Jersey Shore, you must do your best and make the most of every situation.

What you will learn from these early experiences will not be obvious at first, but if you do your best at each and every task you will ultimately look back and see your development and growth. You will have made new friends, picked up some wisdom along the way, and will feel, and actually be, much more prepared for your next job.

I can look back to my first temp job at age eighteen, which lasted only two days. I was helping telephone operators at an international communications company. I remember that I knew nothing about work, but in just two days, a few experienced workers showed me how things worked and I did my best to learn.

When that assignment ended very quickly, I got my second temp job, and already I felt a little more confident. The second job involved not much more than answering phones, filing, and other clerical duties. I kept the position until I started college in September, and I finally felt part of the work world.

Surround yourself with positive people.

Luz King, Information Security Analyst

The key in any job is to do your very best. It won't always be exciting and challenging, but you can make the most of any job by doing whatever it is very well, keeping a positive attitude, showing respect, and asking for more.

A job well done will often lead to your being assigned more challenging and interesting tasks. If you don't do the mundane tasks well, do not expect to be given more responsible work.

Our lives follow a path that we ourselves help fashion. As you grow in age and experience, how you respond to the challenges you are given will begin to mark the way to the next phase. Doing your best at everything leads to the next good thing.

Having one job gives you experience and something more to put on your resume. That, in turn, will lead to the next job, that will likely mean more experience, and so on, and so on. This is the secret of success.

It is really very simple. It is simply cause and effect. If you remember my brief school and work history, the way I gained experience and had a successful career was really quite unremarkable. I followed a path that many of the other successful people quoted throughout this book have taken.

We sometimes accepted jobs that might not have immediately matched our skills or education, but these experiences provided invaluable practice. We worked conscientiously at each job. We took the initiative. We presented a professional image, showed respect for others, and acted in an ethical way. This is the simple, but universal secret of success.

Finding a good mentor, surrounding yourself with positive people in the workplace, and getting a good education complete the equation for success in the workplace. It is totally up to you. Your positive and open response to life and experiences, and your willingness to prepare today for the future, are the keys to winning at the job game.

REFLECTIONS

If you have never worked before, list some of the issues or concerns you have about starting your first job.

_____

_____

_____

Write down how you think you can address these concerns or overcome any anxieties about the workplace.

_____

_____

_____

If you have worked before, list the positive experiences you had and why you think these were positive for you. How did they happen?

_____

_____

_____

If you have worked before, list some of the more difficult workplace situations. State how you handled these situations.

_____

_____

_____

If you did experience some difficult workplace situations, how could you have better approached the issues, based on what you have read in this book?

_____

_____

_____

Do you think you are ready for your first, or your next, job? If yes, state why. If not, state why not.

_____

_____

_____

After reading this book, how prepared do you feel to begin your first, or your next job? What must you do to reach a good level of preparation for work?

_____

_____

_____

Closing Remarks

You are going to love work! You may not like every day of work or everything you do; yet, when you are in the right job you will see beyond the everyday experience and realize you are part of a good thing.

I know this may be hard to believe, since everyone you know probably can't wait until Friday (Thank God it's Friday!) or until their vacations. The truth is that work, while still being work—requiring you to get to bed on time, get up early, commute, and take on responsibility—is really a very rewarding experience.

You will meet new people, including some that will become lifelong friends. You will expand your thinking and have a chance to be creative. Good managers will mentor you and prepare you for your next career step.

As a good employee, you can look forward to improving your lifestyle and making a difference in the world. Every job that exists, no matter how humble, provides a needed service to the world.

The world is waiting for you to lead the next generation. This is a tall order, but your work will give you the opportunity to do your part for the world. You can make a real difference in this world through your work, in ways both big and small. I want to see you succeed in this, because I know you can succeed.

You have innate talents that you will take to the workplace in addition to the skills you gain through education. In this book I have given you the simple but crucial tools to prepare your whole person for the task ahead. Prepare now. Prepare well. Don't get discouraged along the way if obstacles present themselves.

Remember my nephew Joe Slomka? Remember that he had a hard time finding his first job. As he went on to complete his Master of Science degree, he had to prepare himself for the job of his dreams as a color scientist. He refined his skills by working in a small software company, and gained more and more experience and more and more confidence.

After graduation, he also focused on his communication skills, a part of his whole person that needed work. Then he applied for, interviewed, and received a job offer from Sony Pictures Imageworks in Los Angeles.

He was the first person at Sony Pictures Imageworks to have the title of Color Scientist. In less than two years, he used his color science skills in the making of some major motion pictures, including *Spider-Man 3*.

Joe was recruited to his next and current job as Vice President and Principal Color Scientist with the film company, Fotokem. His recent projects have included major motion pictures like *Dunkirk* and *Star Wars: The Last Jedi*.

You will also secure your dream job. Be brave. Be persistent. Be committed to your dream and you are on your way.

Now go, and win the job game!

Suggested Reading and Other Resources

The following list of books and other resources will assist you in strengthening important skills for both school and work, and will assist you in finding work. Your guidance counselor, local library, major bookstores, and internet sites such as amazon can provide many additional resources.

JOB HUNTING

JOB PREPARATION BOOKS

Covey, Sean. *The Seven Habits of Highly Successful Teens*. New York, New York: Fireside, 1998.

DeLuca, Matthew. *Best Answers to the 201 Most Frequently Asked Interview Questions*. New York, New York: McGraw-Hill, 1996.

Fry, Ron. *Your First Interview*. Franklin Lakes, New Jersey: Career Press, 4th Edition, 2002.

Ireland, Susan. *The Complete Idiot's Guide to Cool Jobs for Teens*. Indianapolis, Indiana: Alpha Books, 2001.

BOOKS ON EXPLORING CAREERS

Bolles, Richard Nelson. *What Color is Your Parachute for Teens: Discovering Yourself, Defining Your Future*. Berkeley, California: Ten Speed Press, 2006.

U.S. Department of Labor. *Occupational Outlook Handbook*. Jist Works, Indianapolis, Indiana: 2006-2007.

BOOKS ON BUILDING COMMUNICATION SKILLS

Alba, Cathy. *Speaking Well and Writing Well: Empowering Yourself with "Proper" English: Your Dynamite Guide to Conquering the World.* Wichita, Kansas: Thatch Tree Publications, 2001.

Atlantic Publishing Group. *The Young Adult's Guide to Flawless Writing: Essential Explanations, Examples, and Exercises,* Paperback, 2016.

Davis, Jeanne. *Beyond "Hello": A Practical Guide to Excellent Telephone Communication and Quality Customer Service,* Aurora, Colorado: Now Hear This, Inc. Publishing, 2003.

Ellis, Barbara L. *How to Write Themes and Term Papers—How to Write Successfully in High School and College,* Hauppauge, New York: Barron's Educational Series,* 4th Edition, 2004.

O'Conner, Patricia T. *Words Fail Me,* San Diego, California: A Harvest Book, Harcourt, Inc., 2000.

INTERNET RESOURCES

JOB SEARCH BOARDS

CareerBuilder – National job board to post resumes and search jobs.

Indeed – National job board to search jobs – the most popular job board today for jobs in all industries.

Monster - National job board to post resumes and search jobs.

SnagaJob - A resource for finding local part-time/summer jobs.

ZipRecruiter – National job board to post resumes and search jobs.

PREPARING FOR COLLEGE

College Board - A good resource for the college bound. Provides tips on new SAT process and information on colleges.

FastWeb - A resource for college scholarships, internships, and part-time jobs around the country. Also profiles colleges.

NATIONAL / INTERNATIONAL TUTORING COMPANIES

Club Z – Provides in-home tutoring services for K-12. Club Z will match tutors to the student's personality, learning issues, and academic strengths and weaknesses.

Huntington Learning Center – National company provides tutoring and test prep services for K-12.

Sylvan Learning Centers – Provides high school and college test preparation, as well as individual tutoring services.

Tutor Doctor – Tutoring company, offering in-home tutoring services worldwide. Tutors are matched to the student based on specialty and personality.

ABOUT THE AUTHOR

Beverly Slomka is a former Merrill Lynch executive and currently works as a senior recruiter with Larry White Associates, Inc., a nationwide healthcare search firm. She earned a BA in Psychology and an MS in Education/ Rehabilitation Counseling. She is a member of the Phi Beta Kappa Society, a prestigious society dedicated to academic honors in the liberal arts and sciences. Beverly currently resides with her husband in New York City.